Powerful Places in Scotland

Powerful Places in Scotland

Gary White &
Elyn Aviva

Powerful Places in Scotland

by

Gary White & Elyn Aviva

ISBN: 978-0-9826233-0-5

Library of Congress Control Number:

2010920291

Set in Adobe Caslon Pro 11 pt. and Briso Pro 11 pt., with display in Adobe Caslon Pro in various sizes. Cover and title set in Reliq Std and Briso Pro

Cover photo: Calanais I, Isle of Lewis, Western Isles (Outer Hebrides), by Elyn Aviva.

Contents

Acknowledgments

Gratitude to our mentors and teachers, including Ferran Blasco, Mara Freeman, Juan Li, Sig Lonegren, Anne Parker, R. J. Stewart, and Dominique Susani. Gratitude to all the earth-mystery writers and researchers, including Paul Devereux and Nigel Pennick, who have opened the way for so many others. Gratitude to each other for patience, tolerance, enthusiasm, and inspiration. Gratitude to the land, the stones, the trees, the temples. For those interested in following up with our teachers we offer the following websites:

Ferran Blasco: http://www.zahoriart.com/

Mara Freeman: http://www.chalicecentre.net/

Juan Li: http://www.ichingdao.org/tao/en/biography-of-juan-li.html

Sig Lonegren: http://www.geomancy.org/

Anne Parker: http://latitudewithattitude.com/

R. J. Stewart: http://www.rjstewart.org/

Dominique Susani: http://sacredgeometryarts.com/

Introduction

Over the years we have traveled to a number of unusual places, drawn by curiosity, lured by possibility. Gradually we realized that although many of these sites were interesting, some of them were really powerful. These were places where we felt something out of the ordinary—ranging from a shiver up the spine to an unexpected sense of serenity to a strong intimation that we had entered a "thin place" where the veil between this world and the "other realm" was more easily parted.

What we experienced in these places was an interaction between the energy of the place itself, the human activities at that location (offerings, ceremonies, constructions such as stone circles or temples), and our own openness to experience what was happening at that moment. The feeling that a particular place is powerful can take many forms, and it can be subtle or very strong.

In this guidebook we describe some of the more powerful places we have found in Scotland and invite you to experience them for yourself. We make no claims as to what you may or may not feel when visiting these sites. We have observed that one person may bask in the energy of a particular site, another may feel nothing at all, and a third may want to leave as quickly as possible.

On one visit inside a large, earth-covered passage grave in Ireland, Elyn felt increasingly uncomfortable and shaky but (against her better judgment) stayed to listen to our guide. Afterwards, Elyn took a survey and discovered that several people had left immediately because they felt so ill at ease—and others thought the cairn was a wonderful place in which to meditate. In an isolated monastery in the mountains of Spain, Elyn and Gary were shown into an abandoned chapel. Instantly, they both felt an incredibly unconditional loving presence. Their companion (a very sensitive and intuitive lady) looked at them in puzzlement. She thought the energy in the room was nothing special.

Sometimes our experience has differed on subsequent visits to the same site. We speculate why this may be, but we realize that experiences can never be repeated—whether it's your first taste of a chocolate gelato cone on a sunny day in Rome, or your first kiss, or your first visit to the Grand Canyon. As the Greek philosopher Heraclitus said, "No man ever steps in the same river twice, for it's not the same river and he's not the same man." This is equally true of powerful places.

What makes a place powerful?

The brief answer to "what" is: the land itself has underground water lines, faults or cracks in the earth (sometimes called fire lines), energy vortices, "blind" springs, and so on that our ancestors were able to sense and utilize. An old Gaulish word, *wouivre*, refers to snakes that glide, to rivers that snake through the landscape, and to telluric currents that snake underground from the depths of the terrestrial strata. Experienced dowsers using dowsing rods or pendulums can locate these underground features with great accuracy. If they couldn't, oil exploration and well-digging companies wouldn't waste their money on hiring them.

Our ancestors utilized these energies—and their knowledge of geometry (circles, triangles, pyramid shapes, etc.)—to construct sacred places. For example, an alignment of standing stones may have been placed to draw off energy from an underground fault; a circle of stones may have been built to utilize the energy of an underground spring. The altar of a twelfth-century church may have been carefully placed over the crossing of underground water and fire lines.

How do you sense these energies?

The brief answer to how to sense these energies is: by centering, grounding, and being present to a site *in whatever way works for you.* Feeling the subtle energies that are present in a place requires sensitivity and intuition. It is a bit like tuning a radio dial to a particular frequency. These techniques can be taught (we have studied with several teachers who have taught us how). Such instruction is outside the scope of this guidebook, although we do give a few suggestions for how you can be more attuned to a powerful place.

We encourage you to listen carefully to your own inner guidance as you open yourself to what may be available to you at a particular place on a particular day, at a particular time of day, with the particular predisposition you bring at that moment. You must use your own judgment about what is good or not good for you. Trust your feelings—and enjoy the mystery.

A few more things to notice

Ancient people often constructed several sites at some distance from each other. These sites often appear to have a visual (and probably energetic) relationship to each other and to prominent natural features such as hilltops, gaps between hills, etc. This phenomenon is called "intervisibility" and the landscapes themselves are called ritual landscapes. In other words, a powerful place should be experienced in relationship to its surroundings. Prominent ritual landscapes occur in the areas around the Calanais Stones in Scotland; the alignments at Carnac in Brittany, France; various sites in County Sligo, Ireland; the Nosterfield area in England; and Stonehenge in Wiltshire, England, among others. There is much speculation about the purpose of these landscapes, but it is increasingly clear that they exist and were created intentionally.

Not only were sacred sites constructed with an awareness of the energies of the earth and in relationship to each other and to surrounding natural features—they were also often built to interact with solar, lunar, or stellar events. For example, the light of the setting winter solstice sun shines into the entry passageway of Maeshowe, a site described in this guidebook. Just as churches used to be constructed so that the altar was in the east (facing the rising sun and signifying the resurrected Christ), so were many megalithic sites designed to take advantage of recurring seasonal astronomical events. Unfortunately, it is often difficult to prove which, or how many, events were being marked.

Organization

Each chapter begins with a brief account by Elyn of a visit to a particular powerful place. This is followed by information about the site along with suggestions, quotations, and related graphics. At the end of each chapter are directions on how to get there and a brief space (Notes) for you to add your own observations. The guidebook concludes with a glossary and bibliography.

How did we choose these particular locations? We talked with people; we did research in books and on the web to discover possible powerful places that were not likely to be on every tourist's itinerary; we visited Scotland on several occasions with guides and without; and we paid attention to what we experienced at different sites. We then selected powerful places to include in this guidebook.

This specialized guidebook is not an exhaustive listing of all the powerful places in Scotland; to do that would require a much larger book. Nor is it a complete guide to what to see or where to stay in Scotland. For that you'll need to consult a general travel book. This guidebook *is* intended as an invitation to experience powerful places in Scotland. We hope that it's the beginning of a conversation. We'd like to hear from you.

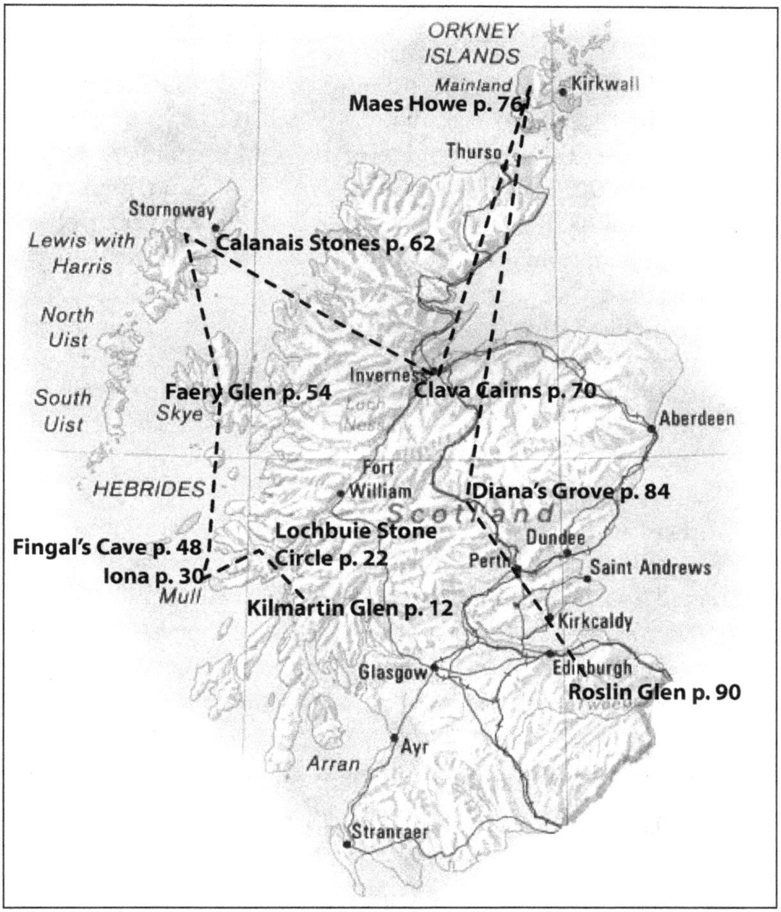

Around Scotland

This map of Scotland presents one possible itinerary to visit the places described in this book. We aren't recommending this as the route of an actual tour, but simply as a way of grouping nearby sites together.

Scotland is a country distinguished by unique landscape and history. One thinks immediately of mountains, islands, and water. The only land border is with

England on the south. Elsewhere it is all sea. There are about 790 islands, many of which are inhabited, and the coastline of the mainland stretches over six thousand miles because of the numerous inlets. The main land mass is crossed by three gigantic faults, one of which has created a series of long, narrow lakes that stretch south and west of Inverness (think Loch Ness Monster), making travel difficult.

"The Earth is, in effect, a giant bar magnet whose geo-magnetic field is constantly changing. Changes in the intensity and also in the orientation of the Earth's field affect the temporal lobes and the pineal gland, both areas of the brain that appear to be involved in the production of dreams, visions and the trance state. These changes often occur at geological fault lines.... Stresses on geological faults create electric and magnetic effects because of the piezo-electricity formed by pressure on the crystals within the rock. In Britain, the places where most of the sacred sites are located toward the west coast—Cornwall, Wales, Cumbria and Scotland—[are] all areas where most ancient sites and ley lines are to be found...." (Mara Freeman, private communication)

Elsewhere there are the mountains of the Northwest Highlands, the Grampian Mountains, and the Southern Uplands. The land has a rugged, primitive beauty that is quite appealing. Most of the population is clustered in the Central Lowlands, which includes the area around Glasgow and Edinburgh. Population density in the rest of the country is very low.

The history of Scotland was summarized by a sixteenth-century wag: "They spend all their time in wars, and when there is no war, they fight one another." The warring clans still hold a powerful place in the Scottish psyche and you will see their colorful tartans everywhere. Scotland has a long, contentious history that you will become aware of as you travel.

Scotland presents the traveler with some unique challenges. Since many powerful places are on islands, travel necessarily requires journeys over water as well as land. The Scottish Tourist Information Centers can be quite helpful in making travel arrangments.

While numerous ferries serve the islands, and they are often coordinated with public bus services, you may encounter some delays and missed connections. Fortunately, a missed connection often leaves you in a place where you can discover unexpected pleasures, so relax and enjoy the journey as well as the destination. If you rent a car, remember that you will be driving on the left side of the road. If you decide to drive, we highly recommend that you purchase a detailed road atlas and/or use a GPS device.

You will note that sometimes we provide alternative spellings for place names. In some cases, Scots-Gaelic spellings have recently taken precedence over more Anglicized versions. We give Scots-Gaelic priority but provide the Anglicized place names as alternatives.

Experiencing a Powerful Place

This is a guidebook about *experiencing* places—not just seeing them. You may have already developed your own way to visit a powerful place. If not, the following may be of use.

Much of the time we humans operate on "automatic," hardly registering where we are or what we feel. Visiting a powerful place is an opportunity to be intentional and alert. In order to fully experience a powerful place, it is important to be present. Really conscious. Really aware of your surroundings and of changes in yourself in response to your surroundings. We suggest an acronym, **BLESSING**, to help remember how to prepare to enter a powerful place—whether it is a forest, a church, or a stone circle.

Going to a powerful place is like getting to know a new friend. Don't rush in. Say "hello." Introduce yourself. Bring a "hostess" gift. Listen politely to what the site has to tell you. Don't be rude or impatient. Don't interrupt. Have a conversation. When you (and it) are finished, don't just leave—remember to say goodbye. And realize that not every powerful place wants to be befriended! Some might be positively taciturn or even grumpy.

BLESSING stands for: **B**reathe slowly and regularly, paying attention to your breath moving in and out. If you have a breathing practice, now is the time to do it. **L**ook and **L**isten within: what are you sensing internally? How do you feel? **E**stablish yourself in your location, perhaps by orienting to the seven directions (east, south, west, north, above, below, and the center within—or, before you, behind you, to your right, to your left, above, below, and the center within). **S**ense your surroundings, opening up your five senses (and sixth sense) to what is around you. **S**tate your **IN**tention to respect this place, to experience what is present. **G**ive gratitude for this opportunity.

In approaching a powerful place, it is very important that we prepare ourselves mentally, emotionally, psychologically, and physically for the experience because what we feel is very much determined by what we bring to the site. Purposeful preparation becomes the prerequisite for having meaningful experiences.

One of our mentors, Mara Freeman, suggests the acronym **ECOLOGY** for remembering how to approach a stone circle. It can, of course, be modified to apply to powerful places in general. "E" stands for **E**ntry, which means enter by first circling the site in a clockwise (sunwise) direction. "C" is for **C**entering yourself. This is often best accomplished by touching one of the stones. "O" stands for **O**ffering, which can be a bit of grain, milk, a strand of hair, saliva, etc., which shows that you come in good faith. The best offerings are biodegradable so they don't linger in the environment to build up over time. "L" is for **L**istening—listen to the sounds around you: birds, wind, wild creatures, and other sounds of nature. "O" stands for **O**pening up your inner and outer senses. "G" is for **G**ratitude to the place, the Earth, all of life, and Nature. "Y" is for **Y**ou: you should leave a place just as you found it. Take nothing and leave nothing. You can see the result of people not observing this injunction at many popular sacred sites: trees damaged by people taking pieces of their bark or carving on them; sites littered with paper wrappers and trash; melted wax dripped over ancient stones. Observe **ECOLOGY**: the Earth and future visitors will thank you.

Elyn Aviva

Inside Nether Largie South Cairn

Kilmartin Glen, Argyll, The Southwestern Highlands

Cairns, standing stones, and prehistoric remains fill a large area near the town of Kilmartin. Visiting the glen is a wonderfully efficient way to experience a wide variety of megaliths—including a unique, one-mile-long alignment of cairns called the Linear Cemetery. We climbed down into the grass-and-stone covered Nether Largie South Cairn. As we sat in the dim light, partially underground, our kilt-wearing guide told us he thought it had originally been a kind of underground kiva, a multi-purpose ceremonial site, later converted into a burial chamber. Leaning quietly against the cool stone walls, I could feel the energy, still palpable 5000 years later. Had people, both living and dead, come here to return to the Mother? I wondered what vision quests, what retreats (temporary or permanent) into darkness had been performed here millennia ago. (Elyn)

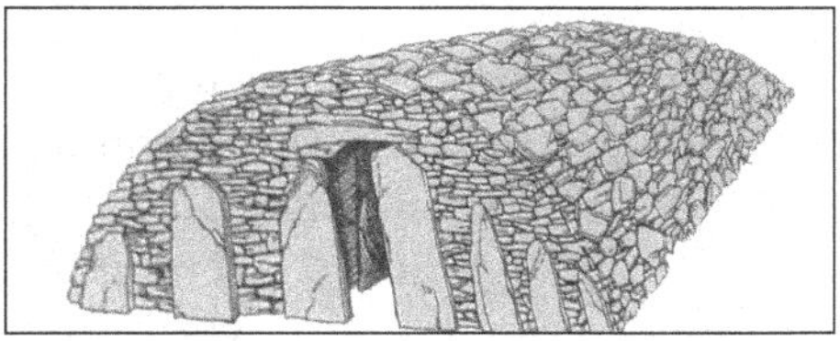

Nether Largie South Cairn as it might have appeared in 3000 BCE

Elyn Aviva

Nether Largie South Cairn today

Kilmartin Glen is one of the richest archeological landscapes in Scotland. Numerous stone circles, cairns, henges, forts, stone carvings, and an abandoned

Templewood Circle as it might have appeared in 3500 BCE

crofters' village are all within a few miles radius. In the village of Kilmartin you can see evidence of human habitation from over 5000 years ago to the present. Six separate sites are an easy walk from each other: Temple Wood Stone Circle (3500 BCE), the three Nether Largie Cairns (3000 BCE), Ri Cruin Cairn (2000 BCE), and Glebe Cairn (1700 BCE). The most impressive is the Nether Largie South Cairn, which can be entered. Look for the faint remains of a large spiral on the side of one of the upright stones in Temple Wood Stone Circle. Perhaps this indicated the entryway.

A number of the stones in these cairns have the "cup and ring" markings that occur in many megalithic sites in Scotland. The "cups" are semi-spherical indentations chipped into the surface of a stone using stone tools. The "rings" are either circles or spirals chipped in the same way and often surrounding the cup. Watch for these features as you walk among the cairns. No one knows why these carvings were made. People have suggested they convey some sort of genealogical information, are maps of the stars, or were used for seasonal ritual offerings. It is clear from the amount of

Elyn Aviva

Templewood Circle today

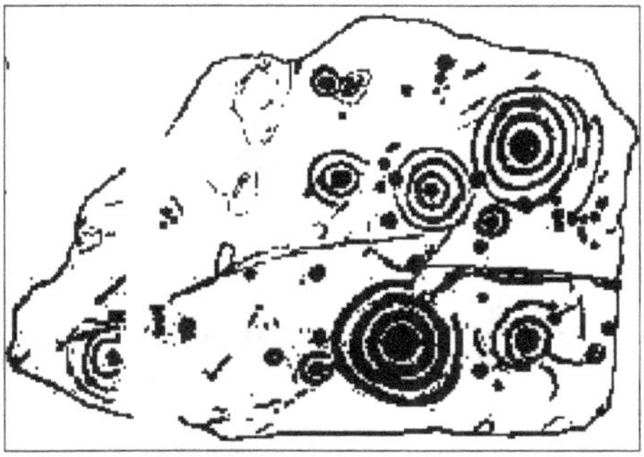

Cup and ring marks

effort required to make them that the cups and rings were significant to those who carved them.

The best way to experience Kilmaratin Glen is to follow the circular route described on the information sign at the entrance. Take some time at each site to explore what it has to offer and enter the Nether Largie South Cairn for a prolonged meditation. You may be able to experience some of the magic that our ancestors felt when the cairn was an important ceremonial center.

"The English author and dowser Paul Devereux calls these sites 'places of geographical sanctity,' the later Romans named the mysterious power found at such places the *genius loci,* or the spirit of the place. A spirit that is still tangible at many Neolithic sites today. Indeed many sensitive people report a subtle but distinct shift in consciousness that occurs when visiting sites such as Stonehenge, Avebury, Silbury Hill, or Newgrange. Therefore the question that naturally arises is this: Does such a shift in consciousness arise as a result of the *genius loci,* the telluric power of such places, or as a result of the symbolic effect of the structure itself? Or, indeed, is it some strange combination of at least those two factors among possible and, as yet, undefined, others?" Tim Wallace-Murphy. *Cracking the Symbol Code: Revealing the Secret Heretical Messages within Church and Renaissance Art.* London: Watkins Publishing, 2005, p. 8.

The cairns were uncovered in the late eighteenth century when farmers were cutting the peat that had made them nearly invisible. The landowners decided to keep the stones in place as an ornamental feature

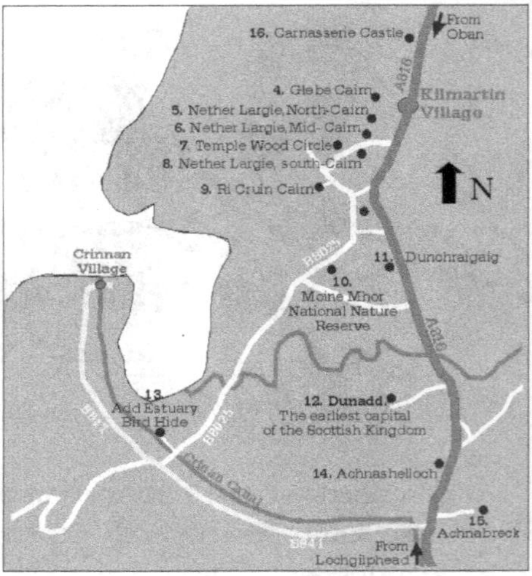

Area map

and oak trees were planted all around them. It was these nineteenth-century romantics who gave them fanciful names like "Temple Wood." Regardless of their motives, we owe these idealists a great debt for preserving the site. Many other megalithic sites were simply dismantled and the stones used to build houses, roads, and walls.

If you are intrigued by scientific explanations, pay a visit to Kilmartin House, a very well appointed local museum. There you will learn what science knows about the megalithic sites and what archeologists found in them. A café in the village serves local specialties.

Elyn Aviva

A cup and ring mark at Achnabreck

The Kilmartin Glen site contains five cairns and one stone circle, along with several standing stones. However, if you want to see the most extensive cup and ring mark-

Elyn Aviva

Climbing Dunadd Hill

ings in Scotland, visit Achnabreck, off A816 in the direction of Lochgilphead. The hill fort of Dunadd is nearby.

Dunadd Hill, near the village of Kilmartin, has been called the original capital of Scotland. This isolated hilltop northwest of Bridgend was fortified during the Iron Age. Around 500 CE it became the site of the capital of Fergus, the first king of Dalriada. There is a carved footprint, a cup mark, and a carving of a boar on a stone slab on top of this hill. The slab may have been a part of the royal coronation rituals of the kings of Dalriada on the west coast of what is now Scotland. The so-called Stone of Destiny, which has been used to crown many English kings, may have been located here at one time. This stone has had a troubled history since it was

Elyn Aviva

The footprint stone on Dunadd Hill

Elyn Aviva

Cross and holy well

taken from Scotland to England in 1296. After many misadventures, it now rests in Edinburgh Castle.

Near Kilmartin Glen is the crofters' village called Kilmory Oib that was abandoned during the infamous "clearing" of peasants from the land in the mid-nineteenth century. A holy well in the center of the village is decorated with crosses on both sides. The west face also has carvings of birds and two discs representing the sun and moon. The well is certainly a powerful place in its own right.

"In becoming *an sith* (pronounced ahn-shee) we align ourselves with what I call the shimmering peace of a place. We open ourselves to its mysteries, not in some romanticized Tinker Bell way but in an authentic dialogue with the holy energies, with the spirits. By entering into such a dialogue with the spirit of peace in a place we are able to experience firsthand the results of inner transformation. We begin to take on and embody the essence of a place of power. Indeed, over time we can become so profoundly merged with a place and identified with its energy that we become part of its spirit, its voice." Frank MacEowen. *The Mist-Filled Path.* Novato, CA: New World Library, 2002, p. 14.

Corryvreckan Whirlpool

Another factor that may contribute to the energetics of the region is the powerful Corryvreckan Whirlpool, which courses through the nearby Gulf of Corryvreckan between the islands of Jura and Scarba. Local legend has it that the hag goddess of winter, Cailleach Bheur, uses the whirlpool to wash out her great plaid. When it is washed completely white she hangs it over the land as a blanket of snow.

The Cailleach Bheur is widely known in the British Isles as the goddess of winter. Depicted as a blue-faced hag, she is reborn every year at Samhain (October 31). She brings the ice and snow of winter and reigns supreme until deposed by Brigit (see Brighid's Well, p. 42) in the spring, eventually turning to stone at Beltaine (May 1). She is an ancient goddess from pre-Celtic times, controlling the seasons and the weather. She is sometimes said to have been born ugly but ends up young and beautiful in the spring. She had seven husbands, each of whom preceded her in death, and fifty foster children who were the beginnings of many races of peoples. In some tales she appears to a knight as a hag asking for love. When the knight accepts her she transforms into a beautiful maiden.

Visiting Kilmartin Glen

Entrance to the glen is free of charge and the site is never closed. Try to arrive early in the day so you will have good light for your visit. The Kilmartin House museum is not free and you should check for open hours before visiting. (http://www.undiscoveredscotland.co.uk/kilmartin/kilmartinglen/)

Map of the area

Getting There

Drive about 30 miles south from the town of Oban to reach the town of Kilmartin. Signs lead to parking areas among the cairns.

Notes

Elyn Aviva

Lochbuie Stone Circle

Lochbuie Stone Circle, near Moy Castle, Loch Buie, Isle of Mull, Inner Hebrides

I fell in love with Mull. How could I not? The twisting main road around the island is only one lane wide, with well-spaced pull-outs to accommodate the occasional bi-directional traffic encounters. I watched with admiration the rhythmic dance of cars, buses, and vans alternately swinging to one side and pausing while another vehicle hesitated and then continued on. I deeply appreciated that the moors, fields, and mountains had been only minimally disturbed by the construction of this only-as-wide-as-necessary road. After all, why build more road than you absolutely need?

Getting anywhere in a hurry was impossible on that kind of road, but eventually we reached Lochbuie and the crumbling vine-entwined Moy castle, partly obscured by protective scaffolding. A short walk past the sheep barns and outbuildings and down a forest trail, we arrived at a nearly undisturbed, never excavated, stone circle in the middle of a field. Eight (at one time there had been nine) splotchy grey stones seemed to be resting peacefully, waiting patiently for whomever ventured this far off the tourist circuit for a quiet visit. (Elyn)

To visit the Western Isles of Scotland is to make a voyage out to the edge. These islands are isolated, not visited by swarms of tourists, and include some of the most beautiful, peaceful country you'll find anywhere. Lochbuie Stone Circle originally contained nine granite slabs, the tallest over six feet in height, with three outlying standing stones of the same ma-

The replacement stone

terial. When one of the stones turned up missing, someone substituted a small round boulder with a hole drilled in its side. The atmosphere of the place is quiet and welcoming. We had the impression that somehow the stones were glad to see us and we, in turn, were very glad to be in their presence.

Researchers have suggested that the three outlying stones are markers for significant solar events. If you stand in the center of the circle and sight over the outlying stones, one stone appears to mark the position of the setting sun at winter solstice, another the setting sun at the cross-quarter days in November and February; the significance of the third stone remains unknown. We wonder why the megalith builders would erect a circle of nine stones for astronomical purposes when a single stone marking the center point would have done. There must have been some other reason for the circle. Depending on where you sight from within the circle, you can find many other possible solar and lunar events—but that doesn't mean they were all intended by the build-

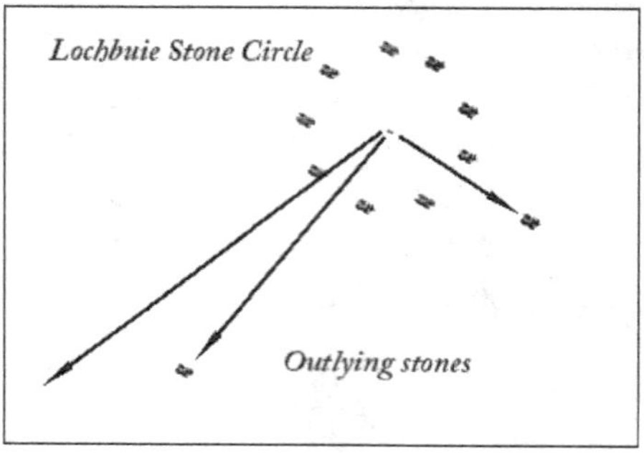

The circle with one of the outlying stones

ers. The circle and outliers were used for something—but what exactly? No one knows.

Lochbuie Stone Circle is located over a great underground fault. Geomancers have pointed out that many megalithic sites are located over underground faults or water. They describe the placement of the stones as resembling earth "acupuncture" and explain that the standing stones draw up energy from the earth and unite it with energy from the heavens—creating, in the case of an activated stone circle, a sort of chalice of telluric-cosmic energies.

Remember the acronyms BLESSING and ECOLOGY (pp 10-11). Spend time with the stones and see what you feel. Perhaps you will connect with the ancient guardians of the stones. The isolation of Lochbuie Stone Circle gives you an opportunity

"Even when we are walking in the countryside, we can all too often become preoccupied with our thoughts, because we keep our minds locked tightly in our brains behind our eyes, affecting how we see—or don't see. The ancients more readily spread out their minds, their memories, their myths, in front of their eyes, in the land. Land was mind, was memory." Paul Devereux. *The Sacred Place*. London: Cassell & Co., 2000, p. 46.

to visit a megalithic site that is little disturbed from its natural state. You are seeing it much as our ancestors might have seen it, though, of course, the climate was considerably different 5000 years ago. This gives the site an authenticity and power that is palpable and well worth the effort it takes to get there.

Among the other sites worth visiting on Mull are MacKinnon's Cave, Duart Castle, Torosay Castle, and the Carsaig Arches, a geological anomaly that left a natural archway carved in stone.

Visiting Lochbuie Stone Circle

The Lochbuie Stone Circle is on private property but access is free. There are no opening or closing times and no signage. Park in the designated area and walk past the castle, following the path to the site, about 350 yards distant.

"At the most basic level, stone is the fabric of the earth, and as such is a symbol of the everlasting. The anthropomorphic view of the world sees stones and rocks as the bones of Mother Earth. They are the fundamental structure that supports all other aspects of physical existence and contains traces of earlier earthly life-forms. This is the outer reflection of our inner fabric, for the bones inside our bodies determine the human physical form. They are the components of the physical body that endure the longest after the spirit has departed. Within the human psyche, stone signifies the eternal substance of existence, at a level deeper than the ego-consciousness. When we touch stone, we commune with this eternal substance, and we feel that the virtues present in the stone are transferred to us." Nigel Pennick. *Celtic Sacred Landscapes.* New York: Thames & Hudson, 1996, p. 39.

Getting There

Mull is part of a group of islands called the Hebrides, off the northwest coast of Scotland. This 150-mile-long chain of islands was once a kingdom in its own right ruled by the Lordship of the Isles. The Inner Hebrides include Islay, Jura, Skye, Mull, Raasay,

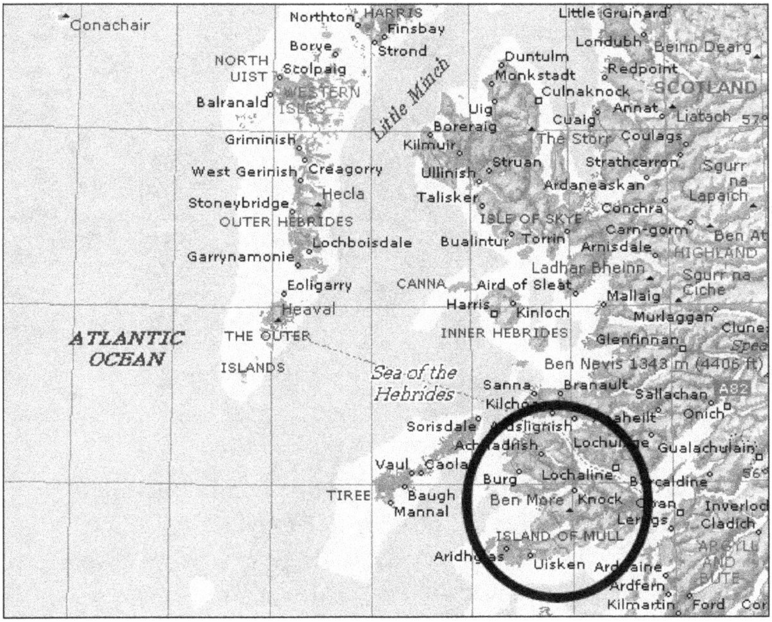

The Hebrides

Staffa, Gigha, Iona, and a number of smaller islands. The Outer Hebrides are Barra, Benbecula, Berneray, Harris, Lewis, North Uist, South Uist, and St. Kilda. The Hebrides have been occupied since 6500 BCE, after the last Ice Age.

If you are coming from the mainland, you can take the auto and passenger ferry from Oban, which ar-

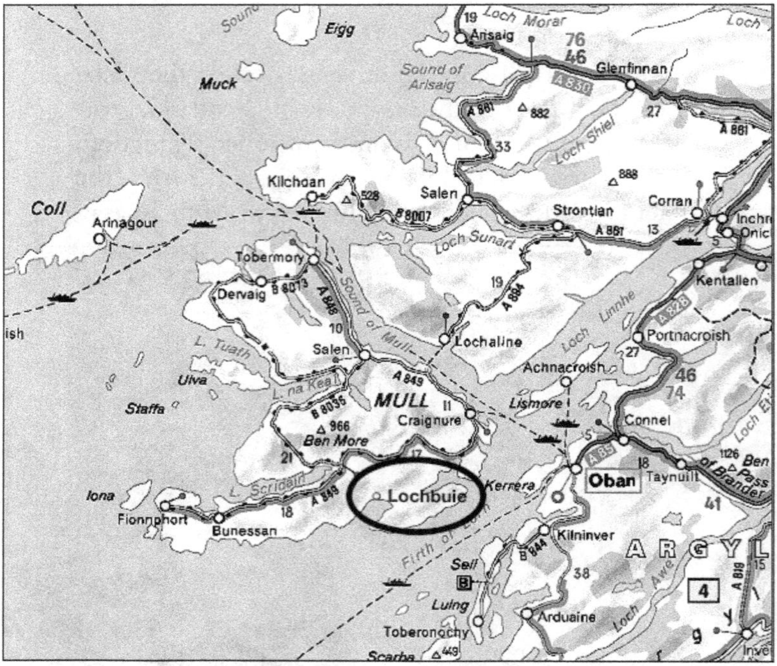

Map of Mull and surrounding islands

rives in Craignure on the island of Mull. This ferry service is operated by the Caledonian MacBrayne line (www.CALMAC.co.uk) and sails several times each day. Consult the website for details. A word of warning: the cutoff time for getting in line to get on the ferry is rigorously observed. Be a minute late and you might not sail.

Once you arrive on Mull you have several choices for getting to the stone circle. If you have brought your own car on the ferry you can drive to the parking lot at the Lochbuie site (get a map of the island in Craignure before starting out). Be prepared to negotiate one-lane roads and observe the various signals you will encounter that indicate who waits for whom at the turnouts. Flashing headlights and hand signals are common. Remember that even on a one-lane road you are driving on the left and will need to pull over to the left.

If you don't have your own transportation there are several ways to reach Lochbuie. You may be able to hire a taxi or you can rent a car on the island. It is also possible to rent a bicycle in Craignure. The most expensive option is to hire a local guide who will take you there and serve you tea. At least six such services are available, which you can find by Googling "Guided Tours on Mull." Another option is to use the local bus service operated by Bowman's Tours (www.bowmanstours.co.uk/) and walk the last miles to the stones. (http://www.undiscoveredscotland.co.uk/areamull/index.html)

Notes

Elyn Aviva

Mara Freeman at MacLean's Cross on the Road of the Dead

Isle of Iona, Inner Hebrides

There's something about Iona. Something about its isolation, its silence—something about the energy of the land.... I can't describe it. I'm not the only one to sense it. It's called "the cradle of Christianity," but in case you're wondering, you don't have to be a Celt or a Christian to appreciate Iona. Spend a few days, not just a few hours, on the land, and you start to slow down, to sink into yourself, to listen quietly to the still small voice within. The cares and concerns of ordinary life drop away, replaced by a deeper knowing, an inner sense.... Describing it is like describing the taste of an orange, the scent of a rose: you have to experience it for yourself. (Elyn)

The tiny island of Iona (only 3.5 miles by 1.5 miles) has a huge history that drips with fable. Take St. Columba wading ashore on the beach at the south of the island with twelve disciples in 565 CE and establishing a monastery that brought Christianity to pagan Scotland. This was not just any monastery: it was a center of learning and the arts that may have created the *Book of Kells*. St. Columba is credited with being able to influence far-off events, control the weather, protect his people against plague, raise people from the dead, change water into wine, etc. Does any of this sound familiar? Some of it is right out of the New Testament. Never mind that he was also credited with shriveling the hand of a disobedient monk, cursing people and ani-

Iona Celtic cross

Iona Abbey before restoration

mals to death, having a voice that struck terror and amazement in his enemies, and burying alive one of his companions in order to hallow the foundations of a chapel.

Saint Columba (521-597 CE), also known as Colum Cille (meaning "Dove of the Church"), was an outstanding figure among the Irish missionary monks who, some of his advocates claim, introduced Christianity to the Picts during the early Middle Ages. Tradition tells us that sometime around 560 CE Columba was involved in a quarrel with Saint Finnian over a manuscript. Columba copied the manuscript at the Irish scriptorium in Clonard Abbey under Saint Finnian, and intended to keep the copy. Saint Finnian disputed his right to the copy and the dispute eventually led to the Battle of Cúl Dreimhne in 561, during which many men were killed. A synod of clerics and scholars threatened to excommunicate Columba for these deaths, but he was allowed to go into exile instead. Columba offered to work as a missionary in Scotland to help convert as many people as had been killed in the battle. He exiled himself from Ire-

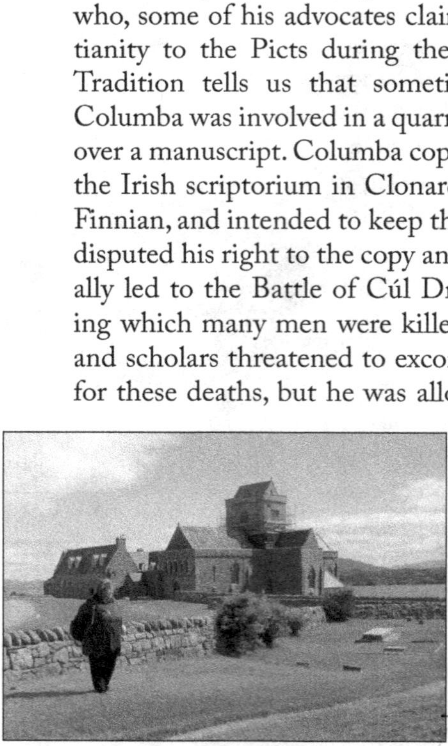

Elyn Aviva

Iona Abbey today

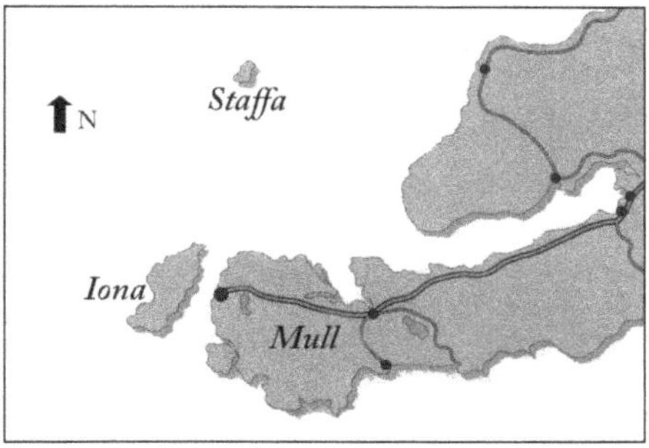

Mull, Iona, and Staffa

land, to return only once, several years later.

The only way to reach Iona is by ferry from Fionnphort on Mull. You sail across the water and come ashore, entering into sacred space and time. The monastery Columba founded has been replaced with Iona Abbey, an imposing thirteenth-century building, restored in 1910, at the foot of Dùn I, the highest point on the island. The abbey may be a part of the mystique—don't miss the beautiful modern cloister—but there are so many other intimations of the sacred that the soul knows that it has come home.

In the next two chapters we describe two of the major sites on Iona—St. Oran's Chapel and St. Brighid's Well on Dùn I—but there are several others worth a half-day walk, including the Fairy Mounds, the south beach, and the nunnery. Buy one of the maps of the island if you plan to make these journeys.

"According to traditional thinking, islands are inherently sacred, being places cut off by water from unwanted physical and psychic influences. From small offshore islets or eyots in rivers to large islands such as Erin and Britain, many Celtic islands have been considered holy. In pagan northern Europe there were a number of smaller islands dedicated to sacred usage. Before their sanctuaries were destroyed by the Romans, the Druids venerated Anglesey. Islands in general were deemed to be under the protection of specific deities, whose shrines existed on and maintained the sacred integrity of the isle." Nigel Pennick. *Celtic Sacred Landscapes.* New York: Thames & Hudson, 1996, p. 105.

The Fairy Mounds

If you walk down the main road south from the ferry landing and turn right on the road that climbs up over a hill, you will be on a road that nearly crosses the island from the east to the west. When the western coast and the gate marking the end of pavement are in sight, you will see a strange-looking mound on your left. This is Sithean Beg, the Small Fairy Mound, a good place for an extended meditation. Just beyond and on the right side of the road is Sithean Mòr, the Large Fairy Mound—also a good place to get in contact with the spirits of the land.

The South Beach

Continuing on past the gate, you will find a trail that leads south across the golf course toward some rather high hills. If you follow that path you will pass a small lake called Loch Staonaig. Continue to the south and you will arrive at the south beach, which legend tells us is where St. Columba first came ashore. This beach is well known as a place to find pebbles of the famous Ionia Marble, a white marble with bright green crystals of serpentine. You will have to search carefully to find these treasures.

The Nunnery

Near the abbey is the ruin of the Iona Nunnery, a Benedictine convent established in 1203. Beathag, daughter of Somerled, was its first prioress. The walls of the nunnery

Elyn Aviva

The eroded Sheela-na-gig

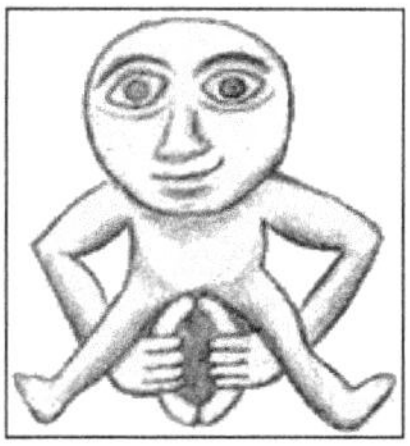
A Sheela-na-gig

are mostly standing, and you can find the carving of a much eroded Sheela-na-gig on the south wall. The nunnery and its gardens are a lovely meditation spot.

Walking from the nunnery toward the abbey you will be following the Road of the Dead, so named because it leads to the cemetery at St. Oran's, near the abbey. Just before a jog in this road you will see Maclean's Cross, which dates from the fifteenth century. This cross is extensively decorated with scrolls, animals, and a mounted warrior at the base.

It is impossible to gain a sense of the riches of Iona with a short visit. Plan on spending at least three or four days if possible. The recommendations we detail below will require that amount of time.

"Sheela-na-Gig comes from the Irish *Sile na gcíoch*, 'Julia of the breasts.' Figurative carving of a naked woman (often emaciated in appearance) squatting with knees apart, one or both hands holding open her large vulva. Sheelas are found carved on Irish, British, and continental European churches built before the sixteenth century; some still remain (especially in Ireland), though most have been destroyed. The Sheela's true origin is unknown and her meaning controversial. Some scholars think she is an ancient good-luck or apotropaic (ward-off-evil) symbol; others suggest she represents fertility; others propose that her off-putting appearance was the Church's effort to discourage lust." Elyn Aviva. *Walking Through Cancer: A Pilgrimage of Gratitude on the Way of St. James.* Santa Fe: Pilgrims Process, Inc., 2009, p. 356.

Visiting Iona

A visit to Iona takes advanced planning. There are only two hotels on the island and they are often fully booked. There are a few other accommodations, which also require reservations, so take care to ensure that you have housing before setting out.

Getting There

The most logical way to get to Iona is by the five-minute ferry ride from the island of Mull. This requires some logistics in itself, since the ferry from the mainland arrives in Craignure on the east side of Mull and the ferry to Iona leaves from Fionnphort on the west (see map on p. 28). This means a car or bus journey from one town to the other. Fortunately, the local buses are well coordinated with the ferry schedules, but you should check the schedules in advance. The ferries are operated by Caledonian MacBrayne (www.CALMAC.co.uk) and the local buses on Mull are operated by Bowman's Tours (www.bowmanstours.co.uk/). This arrangement usually runs smoothly, but local guidebooks constantly warn about disruption of normal services due to weather or other circumstances. Get a copy of the *Travel Guide for the Isles of Mull and Iona* when you land on Mull. It is filled with useful transport information.

If you have rented a car and drive across Mull, please note that tourist cars are not allowed on Iona. You will have to leave your vehicle at Fionnphort.

If making all the arrangements we've just described is not to your liking, there are other options. A number of companies offer package three- and five-day tours from Glasgow, Inverness, and Edin-

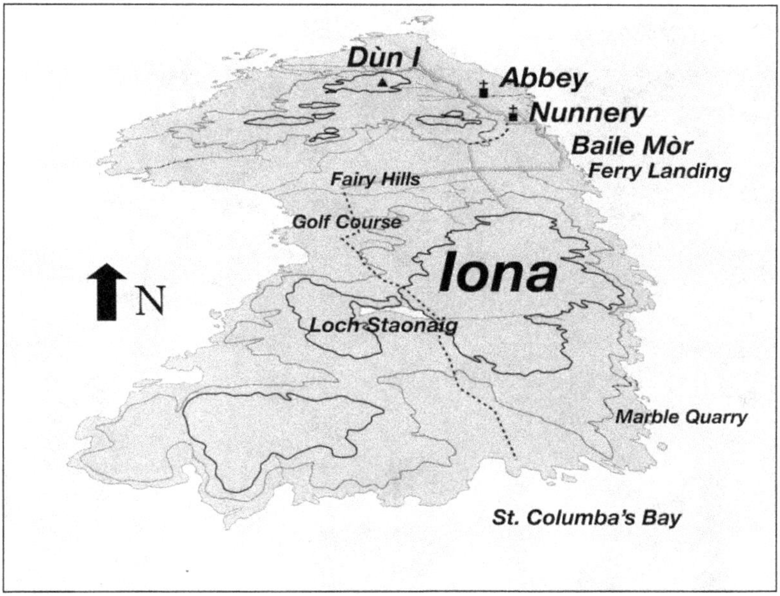

Bird's eye view of Iona

burgh. These allow a day or so on Iona and include other sites, such as Mull and the Isle of Skye. A day or so on Iona will not be enough to see all we suggest but it is better than no visit at all. And, of course, you can always arrange with a touring company to create a private tour if price is no object. (http://www.undiscoveredscotland.co.uk/iona/iona/index.html)

Notes

Elyn Aviva

Doorway into St. Oran's Chapel

St. Oran's Chapel, Iona

It looks like an unassuming little chapel, this one-room house of worship, the oldest building on the island. But strange things happen here. One evening, two women we were traveling with spent an hour singing religious songs in St. Oran's; suddenly they noticed that other voices, one higher, one lower, were joining in. Startled, they looked around; no one else was there. Eyes wide open, voices now a little tight, they kept on singing, enjoying the enhanced harmonies. A little later a woman peered in the doorway and asked who was performing the concert. She was genuinely puzzled to see only the two of them. (Elyn)

Built over St. Columba's original chapel in the twelfth century and restored in 1957, St. Oran's Chapel contains the body and effigy of John, the last Lord of the Isles, who died in 1503. The MacDonald family (The Lords of the Isles) worshipped and were buried here for generations. Gravestones decorate the walls of this simple one-room chapel. Furnishings include an altar, some chairs, a wooden cross festooned with prayer requests written on little pieces of paper (and a bowl with paper and pen in case you wish to add your own request), and a few kneeling benches. The stone floor and plastered stone walls give the small space an acoustical resonance that invites you to sing. A few voices will fill this space—even without the participation of unseen forces. If you are inspired to sing or chant, listen carefully to the effect of your voice in the room. There is magic here.

There is much folklore about St. Oran's Chapel. In one version of the tale (which seems to reflect ancient Celtic practices), St. Columba said to his monks, "It is well for us that our roots should go underground here . . . It is permitted to you that one of you go under the earth of this island to consecrate it." Oran (one of St. Columba's monks in the story) responded, "If thou wouldst accept me, I am ready for that." Columba said, "O Oran, you shall receive the reward of this: no request shall be granted to anyone at my tomb, unless he first ask of thee." Oran was interred alive and after three days Columba ordered the grave opened. Oran immediately opened his eyes and exclaimed, "There is no such great wonder in death, nor is Hell what it has been described." At this, Columba exclaimed, "Earth, earth, on Oran's eyes, lest he gossip further." and poor Oran was buried once again.

> "Various themes can be teased out of this extraordinary tale (St. Oran's burial). On the one hand, it is an example of the widespread folkloric motif of the 'can't be built church,' in which the holy building cannot be erected in one spot because it displeases the fairies, or the Devil, or another supernatural entity. Either the church has to be moved to another spot or the demonic force is overcome in some appropriately Christian manner. In addition, some writers have linked Oran's volunteering to die with the Celtic-Druidic practice of the willing sacrifice. Several Iron Age 'bog bodies' found in the British Isles were high status victims who had lived a good, indeed luxurious life before their (presumably willing) death . . ." Geoff Holder, *The Guide to Mysterious Iona and Staffa*. Tempus Publishing Limited, 2007, p. 39.

In another version of this tale there was difficulty in building the monastery and Oran was sacrificed to allow construction to continue. No matter which tale you prefer, the gist of it is that this place is indeed one of the so-called "thin places," which may account for the strange occurrence Elyn related above.

St. Oran's before restoration

Just outside the chapel is St. Oran's Graveyard, also called Reilig Odhráin, a grass-covered mound that supposedly contains the graves of many clan chiefs from the Hebrides, eight Norse kings, four Irish kings, and forty-eight Scottish kings. A recent addition is the grave of the former leader of the Labour Party, John Smith, who died in 1994. The road that connects the Nunnery with St. Oran's Graveyard is known as "the Street of the Dead" and is marked by MacLean's Cross, a mighty fifteenth-century high cross.

Guidebooks describe Iona Abbey (next to the chapel) as the main attraction on the island. It is an impressive place, but if you want to experience a very special energy, don't miss St. Oran's Chapel. You may also find that Reilig Odhráin is a powerful place to meditate and connect with the wisdom of ancient kings.

Visiting St. Oran's Chapel

The chapel is open at any reasonable hour. (http://www.undiscoveredscotland.co.uk/iona/storanschapel/index.html)

Notes

Elyn Aviva

Brighid's Well of Eternal Youth

Brighid's Well of Eternal Youth, Dùn I, Iona

Bridget, Brigit, Brighid, Bride—her name changes with the landscape, but her protective presence remains. The "Exalted One," the "Bride of the Isles," Celtic goddess of poetry, smithing, childbirth, healing, fire and hearth, she gradually morphed into a Christian saint, also known as the midwife/foster mother of Jesus or "Mary of the Gaels." Loving and maternal, she is remembered still at the triangle-shaped sacred spring hidden behind an outcrop of stone on the summit of Dùn I, the "Hill of Iona," the highest point on the island.

St. Bridget

I clambered up the rocky trail, past a commemorative cairn, heading toward the top. Far below my feet were green fields and white-capped waves, startlingly blue water, and, in the distance, the Isle of Staffa, dark and resonant. I walked around a large granite outcropping and found the spring nestling beneath the sheltering rocks, its fresh, cool waters rich with peat. The sky reflected bronze on the gently rippling surface. Sitting quietly, I felt the presence of long-gone worshippers and ancient prayers—and, perhaps, of Brigit herself. (Elyn)

This triangular pool near the top of Dùn I is known by various names: the Fountain of Youth, the Well of Age, the Well of Beauty, as well as Bride's Well and the Pool of Healing. It is reputed never to have run

Bridget's cross

dry, even in times of extreme drought. The Scottish writer Fiona MacLeod (the pseudonym of William Sharp) wrote that s/he climbed Dùn I because, "if anywhere, I thought that from there I might see the Divine Forges, or at least might discover a hidden way, because of the power of that water, touched on the eyelids at sunlift, at sunset, or at the rising of the moon . . ." A local legend asserts that good luck will come to anyone who ascends the mountain seven times. Another belief is that the water has the power to return one to a youthful appearance.

The legend of St. Bride (BREEJ-uh) caring for the baby Jesus is associated with this spring. Here the Celtic young maid, Bride, rescued a young lamb from a falcon, the lamb resting in her arms while the falcon sat peacefully on her shoulder. An energy vortex opened and Bride was transported to Bethlehem on the eve of Christ's birth, where she acted as midwife and stayed with the Holy Family, acting as nursemaid to Jesus for a year and a day. Then she was returned to Iona by angels.

St. Bride returned to Iona by angels, by John Duncan, 1913

These stories underline the fact that this place is another one of Iona's "thin places," where the "other realms" and this realm are more likely to

St. Bride

intersect, where ordinary space and time relations are suspended. We have had experiences at this site that confirm this. It is a wonderful place to spend an hour or so in meditation and contemplation. By the way, in spite of its dark appearance, many consider the water safe to drink. Others take Fiona MacLeod's suggestion and touch their eyes or bathe their faces in this water.

Visiting Brighid's Well

Dùn I is open at all times with no admission fees. There are no roads on Dùn I so there is no alternative to walking up to the spring. It is a fairly strenuous but short hike, so prepare with proper shoes and take along a supply of water. Those with physical disabilities should be cautious about trying to climb the hill. (http://www.mythicalireland.com/mythology/tuathade/brighid.html)

Elyn Aviva

A Bridget's cross floating in the spring

"The process of reanimating the world with sacredness is rooted in opening ourselves to the energies of the divine feminine. The Celtic tradition is replete with expressions and examples of the divine feminine. As an archetype and a tangible energy, the holy feminine has deep roots in the Celtic psyche, and she wears many faces. Sometimes the sacred woman expresses herself as an initiatory power, as in the primal Scottish tradition of the goddess Scathach, who trained warriors, such as the great Irish warrior of Ulster, Cuchulain, how to fight. At other times the holy feminine is reflected in healing, midwifery, and poetic inspiration, such as with Brighid. Whether as initiator, healer, midwife, or guide, the Celtic spirit in both men and women openly embraces the feminine." Frank MacEowen. *The Mist-Filled Path*. Novato, CA: New World Library, 2002, p. 155.

Getting There

It would be wise to purchase a detailed map of the island, available in the gift shops or at local hotels. Take the road past the abbey toward the north of the island (see map on p. 37). You will pass a gift shop on the left. A little further, a sign on a gate on the left announces the trail to Dùn I. Walk this trail to the top of the mountain, continuing around the summit to the right. The spring is down a slope and hidden behind a prominent rock outcropping. It is not well marked

Elyn Aviva

The gate to Dùn I footpath

but a trail goes directly to it. The view from this point is outstanding.

Notes

Elyn Aviva

The view from the inside of Fingal's Cave

Fingal's Cave, Isle of Staffa, North of Iona

The boat rocked and tipped as we sailed from Iona to the Isle of Staffa. From a distance, Staffa reminded me of an immense dark soufflé, the lower half vertically ridged, the upper half rounded and crusty. Our boat pulled up to the minimalist pier and we disembarked. A twisting stone trail leads to the grass-covered island top, but instead of venturing up we ventured sideways on The Causeway that leads to Fingal's Cave, a gaping, water-sloshed cavern bored into the island by the sea. I felt like a Lilliputian walking over the tops of huge columnar-basalt crystals, truncated at different heights.

Once inside Fingal's Cave, I leaned against the wall and looked around. Above me, behind me, before me were glistening, greenish-black basalt columns. I was inside a stone cathedral constructed not by humans but by nature. And like a well-constructed cathedral, it has impressive acoustics. Perched on the narrow ledge that runs along the side of the cave, high above (at least for now) the very deep blue sea, my companions and I sang "Amazing Grace" to the surrounding rocks. I think I heard them listening. (Elyn)

Fionn MacCoul

Fingal's Cave is named after the third-century Irish hero Fionn MacCoul, who is said to have had his headquarters on the island. The unique and dramatic appearance of the huge vein of columnar basalt (the same stone that makes up the Giant's Causeway in Ire-

Nineteenth-century engraving showing Fingal's Cave as a cathedral

land and the Devil's Tower in Wyoming) and the size of the cave (60 feet high, 50 feet wide, and 230 feet deep) have made it a popular tourist destination for nearly two centuries. The columnar basalt was created from molten lava 60,000,000 years ago. As the liquid stone congealed, it formed myriad polygonal crystals that resemble organ pipes stacked upright. They range in diameter from eight inches to over three feet.

The cave was first described by British naturalist Sir Joseph Banks in 1772. He wrote, "Compared to this, what are the cathedrals and palaces built by men? Mere models or playthings, imitations, as his works will always be when compared to those of nature." Queen Victoria visited in 1847 and wrote, "The effect was splendid, like a great entrance into a vaulted hall: it looked almost awful as we entered." Felix Mendelssohn visited in 1829 and was so impressed that he wrote his "Hebrides Overture" (also called "Fingal's Cave") in 1832. This popu-

A slightly more realistic drawing of the cave

lar orchestral work has made the name Fingal's Cave known throughout the world.

The power of this place comes from its monumental size and isolation, along with the amazing acoustical properties of the cave itself. Sounds are amplified by the cave along with the sounds of the breakers crashing against the cave walls. The effect is strange and otherworldly.

There are those who believe that the vibrations emanating from Fingal's Cave cross the bay to bathe

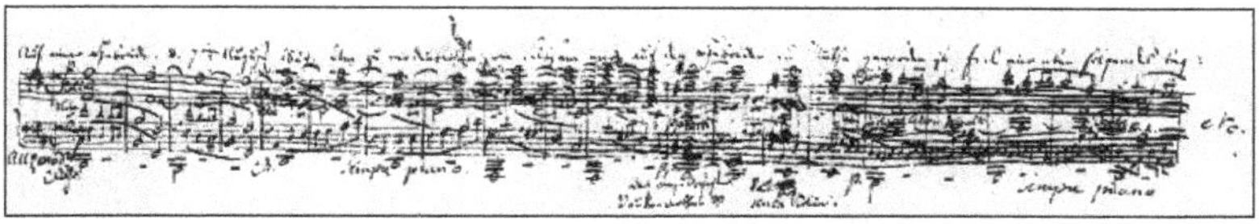

Mendelssohn's original sketch for "Hebrides Overture," contained in a letter to his sister, Fanny

Iona in a special energy. Fingal's Cave is in direct line with Iona, so there may be something to this esoteric notion.

At one time the island was inhabited. In 1800 there were three red deer on the island, later replaced by goats, a small herd of black cattle, and later by sheep, but in 1997 all livestock was removed. This has led to a regeneration of the island's vegetation. Puffin, black-legged kittiwakes, common shag, and gulls nest on the island and the surrounding waters, providing food for gray seals, dolphins, basking sharks, minke, and pilot whales.

Visiting Fingal's Cave

You can walk into the ocean-filled cave in good weather by following the well-marked path along the causeway from the boat dock. The stones can be quite slippery when wet, so be sure to wear sturdy shoes with good rubber soles. It is possible to walk nearly to the back of the cave if the tide is low, but that requires climbing under the chain that clearly marks the end of the official route. The acoustical effects are well demonstrated without going that final hundred feet. (http://www.scotland-inverness.co.uk/staffa.htm)

Getting There

Boats leave several times daily from Fionnphort on Mull and the boat dock on Iona in good weather. There are four-hour trips that go only to Staffa as well as trips that include other islands. These tours give you about one hour on the island. Landing on Staffa can be easy, difficult, or impossible, depending on sea conditions, so it is best to check with the operators in advance. Sailings also depend on demand, so it is best to book in advance even in good weather. Two websites that will provide information are www.staffatrips.co.uk and www.staffatours.com.

Notes

Elyn Aviva

Castle Ewen in the Fairy Glen

Fairy Glen (Glen Conon), near Uig, Trotternish Peninsula, Isle of Skye, Inner Hebrides

As we walked into the Fairy Glen, white-fleeced, black-faced sheep trotted out to watch our passing. Were they fairy sentinels, I wondered, unsure what to expect in this strange landscape of hills and hollows. Peculiar conical mounds surrounded us, their bright green sides layered and textured in concentric rings. All green, all green—grass and fern and leaf—broken only by exuberant clumps of purple-pink, bell-flowered foxglove. In the distance, the tower-like rock formation called Castle Ewen beckoned us to climb its craggy sides.

The further we walked the more evocative the glen became. Groves of hazel and rowan shaded a crumbling stone wall where we rested and spoke of magical things and fairy legends. Then, on and up to the side of Castle Ewen butte, to walk a stone spiral built by human—or fairy?—hands. Meditating in the field below, I felt something watch me from behind a boulder.... (Elyn)

If this is your idea of fairies you'll likely be disappointed.

Don't look for the Fairy Glen on the Isle of Skye in your Scottish travel guides. It won't be there. Neither will it be on most maps you can buy. Even local sources barely mention it, so it will not be overrun with tour-

Elyn Aviva

Hazelwood in the Fairy Glen

ists. This is a very strange and evocative landscape. Numerous small conical hills dot the area, all with concentric rings running around them. Small lakes, groves of hazel and rowan trees, ancient stone walls crumbling into the earth, a fairy castle that can be climbed; rustling grass and fluttering fern complete the scene. The place looks like a set for a Walt Disney movie but it is entirely natural. Human hands had little or nothing to do with its creation.

The Fairy Glen lies hidden on the Isle of Skye. To further deepen the mystery, the name "Skye" has nothing to do with the sky. It is derived from the Norse word *ski*, which means "cloud," and *ey*, which is "island." So Skye is really the Cloudy Island, or, as it is known

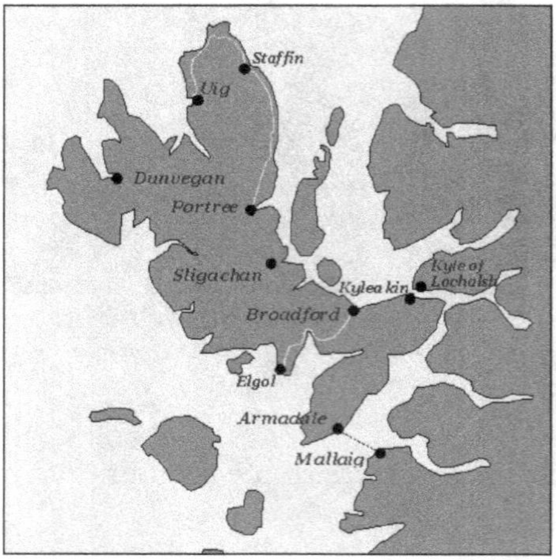

The Isle of Skye

The Old Man of Storr rock formation

worldwide, "Eilean a' Cheo"—the Misty Isle. Skye is the largest island in the Inner Hebrides. It is about 50 miles long and 25 miles wide at its broadest point. It has 350 miles of coastline and is approximately 350,000 acres in size, an island with several large peninsulas. The Fairy Glen is on the northeastern peninsula, called Trotternish, just south and east of the town of Uig.

Other Things to Do

The Isle of Skye is one of the primary tourist destinations in Scotland. Millions of people visit every year, and there is much to do. You can visit Dunvegan Castle, see the rock formation called the Old Man of Storr, sample single-malt whisky at Talisker Distillery, cruise the other Western Islands, or just relax on this peaceful, beautiful island.

Dunvegan Castle is the seat of the Clan MacLeod. It is the oldest continuously inhabited castle in Scotland and has been the stronghold of the clan chiefs for nearly 800 years. Originally designed as a fortress to keep people out, it was first opened to visitors in

Elyn Aviva

Dunvegan Castle

1933. The rooms in the castle display a number of important clan relics. Chief among them is the Fairy Flag of Dunvegan. Various legends describe its origins and magical properties. The flag has been examined numerous times over the last two centuries, and it appears to be Syrian silk, woven between 400-700 CE. The elaborate gardens are a pleasure to explore, and seal-spotting trips depart from the nearby jetty.

You can also visit the Fairy Bridge on the Isle of Skye, said to be related to the Fairy Flag of Dunvegan. It seems that a young chief of the clan MacLeod fell in love with a fairy princess. They were determined to marry but the king of the fairies forbade it. The young fairy princess was so distressed that the king finally relented and agreed to a period of "handfasting," a form of trial marriage that traditionally would last for a year and

Elyn Aviva

The Fairy Bridge

day and was common among Celtic people. However, the king demanded that at the end of the handfasting the princess must return to her own people and take nothing human with her.

The couple lived in harmony and soon a young son was born to them. At the end of a year and a day the couple parted with great sorrow at the Fairy Bridge and the princess returned to her kingdom. As she left she made her husband promise that their son would be well cared for and never allowed to cry, for the sound of his cries would cause her untold grief, even in the far-away fairy realm. The chief kept his promise and the young MacLeod was never left unattended and never allowed to cry.

However, on the occasion of a birthday celebration for the chief, the young nursemaid assigned to take care of the infant crept from the room to watch the party. Unattended, the baby began to cry. The child's mother heard the cries and suddenly appeared by his side. She took up the young baby and cradled him back to sleep, covering him with her fairy shawl. Then she disappeared. The shawl became the Fairy Flag of Dunvegan.

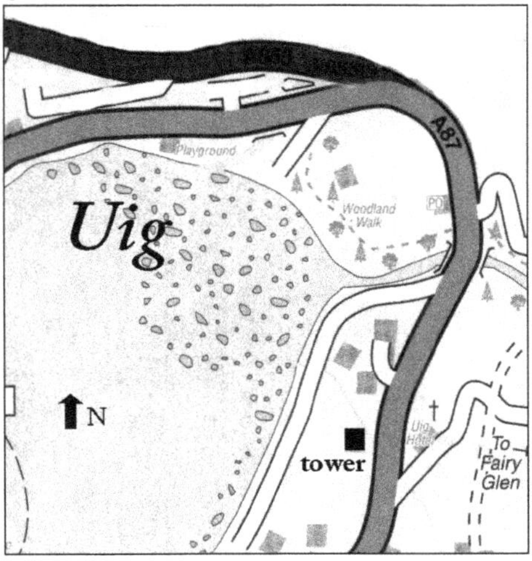

Visiting the Fairy Glen

The Fairy Glen is open at all times. There is no admission and no one is guarding the gate because there isn't one. Take the A87 toward Uig and turn on the road to Balnablock. There is a tower on the left at the turn off. Park your car, either closer or farther away depending on how energetic you feel. Then start to walk, keeping to the road or getting off it and going cross-country. The glen is best viewed on foot. You'll see Castle Ewen on the right side of the road. Bear in mind that this is a very moist climate so waterproof footwear is highly

Map of the Isle of Skye

recommended; keep your rain gear close by. (http://www.scotland-inverness.co.uk/skye.htm#sights)

Getting There

You can drive to the Isle of Skye by crossing the Skye Bridge between Kyle of Lochaish on the mainland to Kyleakin on the island. This toll bridge, which was opened in the 1990s, has brought considerable development to the island. The more traditional way of getting to Skye is by auto/passenger ferry from Mallaig on the Scottish mainland to Armadale on the island. The ferry is operated by Caledonian MacBrayne (www.CALMAC.co.uk). It is essential to book in advance.

Once on the island you can rent a car in Broadford or Portree and drive to the Fairy Glen. Driving is the only reasonable way of getting there. You will also need a car to visit most other attractions on the island. Or, as always, you can schedule a private tour.

Notes

Elyn Aviva

The Calanais Stones

Calanais I (Callanish Standing Stones), Isle of Lewis, Western Isles (Outer Hebrides)

What is it about these 49 standing stones that brings us back again, traveling once more to the remote Western Isles to stand beside them at sunrise and dusk, to walk next to them and rest beside them? Mute and mysterious, they only gradually, grudgingly give up their secrets—and then only to the persistent, and then only little by little. I ponder the equal-armed Celtic cross they form, the ruined dolmen in the center, the uneven avenues of stones and odd-turned megaliths. Is there significance in their jagged edges and uneven tops? Hard to know how much is intentional, how much is circumstantial. I feel their mystery, their energies shifting and changing with the cycles of the seasons, part of a sacred landscape marked on hilltop and notch, bringing heaven down to earth by marking celestial movements on the land.

In 2006 we came here for the once every 18.6 year Lunar Major Standstill, an astronomical event supposedly marked by a gap in the standing stones. It was a rare opportunity to experience Calanais as it might have been experienced 4000 years ago. We were not alone in our desire. Hundreds of colorfully dressed young people chanted and drummed to the full moon as it skimmed the horizon. A Church of Scotland youth choir sang hymns to fend off the encroaching pagan darkness. (Elyn)

The Isle of Lewis is the northern part of Lewis and Harris, the largest island of the Outer Hebrides. Lewis is, in general, the lower-lying and more fertile part of the island; Harris is more mountainous. Lewis

Elyn Aviva

The Stones of Calanais

contains the only town, Stornoway, and three-quarters of the population of the Western Isles. Lewis is famous for its large collection of megalithic sites, including the Standing Stones of Calanais. They are also known as Callanish, but Calanais is the currently preferred Scots-Gaelic spelling. The sites are given Roman numerals, with the central and most important site called Calanais I.

Calanais I is an extraordinary monument, an ancient (and contemporary) center of power. It is the epicenter of a nexus of stone circles and other megalithic sites, mostly located within sight of it. Together they form an extensive ritual landscape.

The site has been known locally for many generations. Around 1680 John Morisone wrote, "It is left by traditione that these were a sort of men converted into stone by ane Inchanter: others affirme that they were sett up in places for devotione." Martin Martin, who visited Calanais around 1695, reported that "they told me, it was a Place appointed for Worship in the time of Heathenism. . ."

The Calanais Stones as men converted into stone

By the mid-nineteenth century

An early drawing of the stones. Note that peat was still being cut when this drawing was made.

the area was covered with peat to a depth of five to six feet, which nearly covered the shorter stones. It was only when the peat was removed in 1857 that the true nature of the site was revealed. The circle was often thought to be the work of Druids, until the actual age of nearly 5000 years was established, long before the time of the Druids. Calanais was held in private hands until 1885, when it was taken into government protection. In 1939 it was deeded to the government and is maintained by Historic Scotland, http://www.historic-scotland.gov.uk/

Another early drawing in which the central circle is still partially covered with peat.

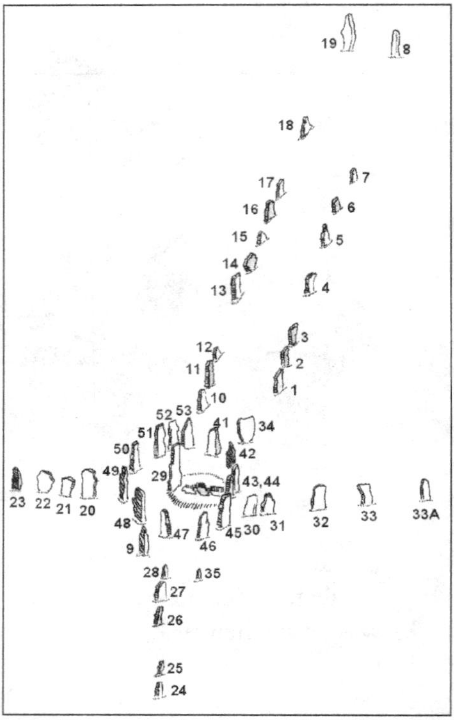

The stones as numbered by Admiral Somerville in 1912

The site contains 13 primary stones that form a flattened circle 43 feet in diameter. Within this circle are one very tall stone and the remains of an early passage tomb of later origin. Extending from the circle is a series of four alignments in roughly a north, south, east, and west direction. The overall layout resembles a Celtic cross, but it predates the appearance of Celtic Christianity by millennia. The alignment on the north is a double line of stones that form an avenue. There are 49 granite schist stones in all. A feature of many of these stones is, oval inclusions of black hornblende.

"Well, the earth is a person—a goddess and we are part of her—in her. Now just as in our bodies there are certain parts which are more in contact with impressions than others, like the eyes, or perhaps the ears, so it is with the earth. There are certain places in her body which are sensitive, and beings, strangers to us, can manifest more easily in those places." AE, spoken to Edith Lyttleton.

As with other megalithic sites, there has been much speculation about the original purpose of Calanais I. In recent times it has been proposed that the stones may have been erected, in part, to view the Lunar Major Standstill. Every 18.6 years the full moon traverses a very low track along the horizon; if there are hills on the horizon, the moon will appear to set and rise several times. Such is the case at Calanais I.

On the horizon south of Calanais I is a series of hills known locally as the "Sleeping Beauty" because they resemble a reclining female form. The moon rises above and sets behind these hills at the Lunar Major Standstill. We witnessed the phenomenon in 2006 and can attest to this effect. However, the relationship between this event and the stones remains to be proven. Much depends on the viewing location—and there is no clear indication of the proper location within Calanais I. Researchers have demonstrated many other astronomical alignments for the stones,

"The perception of a female form in the landscape reaches back to the Stone Age. From Callanish, an important group of stone circles on the Scottish Isle of Lewis, the eastern skyline is occupied by the Pairc Hills and resembles the form of a reclining woman. Sometimes called the 'Sleeping Beauty,' her Gaelic name is *Cailleach na Mointeach,* the Old Woman of the Moors, a pseudonym for the Hag or Earth Mother. She is well known to the present inhabitants of the Callanish area and was doubtless so to the people who built the stone circles. Every 18.61 years, the time in the lunar cycle known as the Major Standstill, the moon rises out of the hills as if the Earth Mother is giving birth to it, and skims the horizon appearing to set amongst the stones. Further south is the Scottish island of Jura, which has a range of mountains called the Paps ('Breasts') of Jura, on account of two rounded, breast-like peaks in their midst. The summer solstice sun appears to set into the Paps when viewed from the standing stones group at Ballochroy on the Kintyre peninsula. To experience sight lines like this is to feel for a moment that one is seeing through the eyes of Stone Age people." Paul Devereux. *Earth Mysteries*. London: Judy Piatkus Ltd., 1999, pp. 121-122.

but they are difficult to prove irrefutably. Several psychics have proposed that it is a sort of transformer of energy and intention. Spend some time among the stones and see what *you* think.

It is clear that the numerous Calanais sites form an intervisible landscape and are probably energetically as well as visually connected. Each site should be experienced in relationship to its surroundings. In addition, it is important not only to look at the stones in a site but also at the space *between* the stones. This change of focus can be quite revelatory.

Visiting the Calanais Stones

The Calanais I site is free and open to the public at all reasonable hours. An excellent visitors' center south of the site offers a restaurant, a bookstore, and restrooms, along with an interpretive film about the site.

Getting There

Auto/passenger ferries sail from Ullapool to Stornoway and from Uig, Skye, to Tarbert. They are operated by Caledonian MacBrayne (www.CALMAC.co.uk). There are scheduled flights from Aberdeen, Benbecula, Edin-

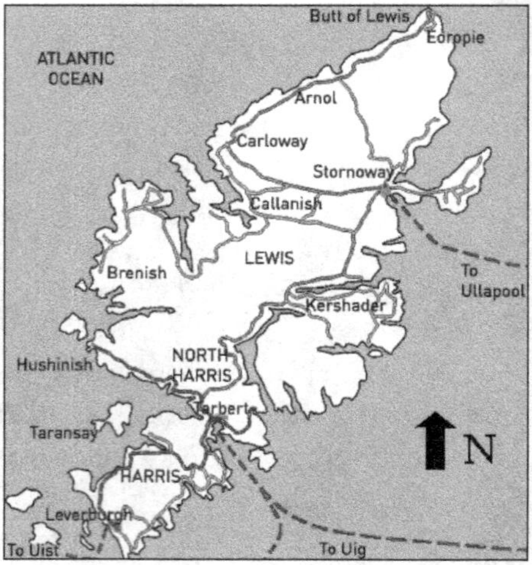

The isle of Lewis

burgh, Glasgow, and Inverness to Stornoway Airport. Once on Lewis you can rent a car or bicycle in Stornoway. (If you plan to reach the stones by bicycle you should be a strong rider; it is a long trip.) Tours are offered by several agencies. Google "Tours to Lewis, Scotland" to see what is offered. Lewis/Harris is really out on the edge, but local accommodations are quite comfortable. (http://www.undiscoveredscotland.co.uk/lewis/calanais/index.html)

Notes

Elyn Aviva

Clava III

Balnuaran of Clava (Clava Cairns), Inverness, The Highlands

Suddenly everything became quite still as I walked slowly within the sheltering grove of beech trees. I contemplated the three rubble-topped Clava cairns, their central chambers delineated with varicolored boulders, some glittering with mica and quartz. An outer ring of standing stones surrounds each of them, creating a visual echo of their circular shape. Two of the cairns are so-called passage tombs, but one has no entrance and no exit. Tombs? Surely they were much, much more, carefully oriented toward the midwinter solstice sunset. At some point the chambers were covered with rubble, as effective as a modern "Out of Business" sign. Why were they built 4000 years ago? How were they used? Who decorated the stones with deep-etched cup marks and abstract designs? Only watchful silence greeted my questions. (Elyn)

The Balnuaran of Clava site contains three large stone circles with distinctive central chambers and a surrounding curb of upright stones. Evenly spaced standing stones form an outer ring around each one. Two of the cairns (those on the north and south of the site) have passages that lead outward from the central chamber in a southwestern direction, which aligns with the midwinter sunset. The third, which is in the center, has no such passage.

It appears that the cairns with passages were covered at one time, perhaps with corbelled stone roofs, as are many other megalithic sites in Europe. It seems likely, however, that the center cairn may have been left open and could have been used for a different purpose than those on the north and south. In recent years the top of the northern cairn has been covered with a tarpaulin at midwinter sunset; sunlight dramatically pierces the passageway and shines on the back wall. A fourth feature of the site is a single small circle of stones that may be of later construction.

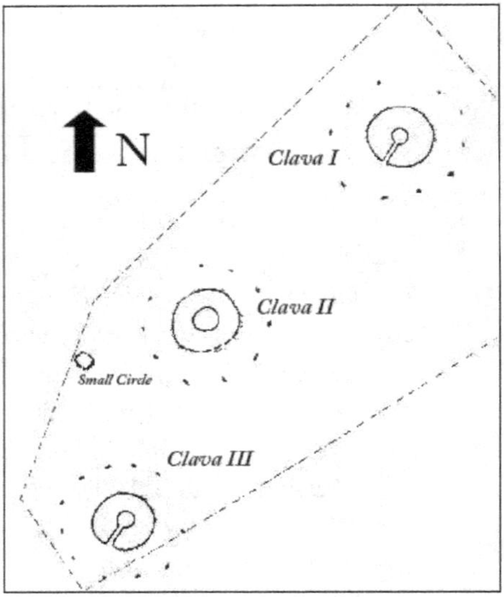

The Balnuaran of Clava site plan. Notice the three large circles with outlying stone circles and the small circle between Clava II and Clava III

A distinctive feature of these cairns, along with the outside circle of stones, is that the space between the inner and outer circles has been completely filled with smaller stones. In the center cairn, Clava II, the filler stones create a pattern of four sections of contrasting color and texture. As if to emphasize this unique "pinwheel" effect, lines of stones lead out from the circumference to the outer circle of standing stones.

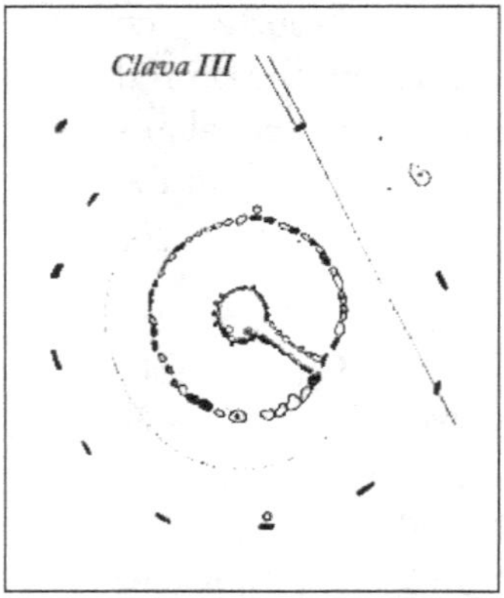

Clava III showing the fence and road cutting through the outer circle.

Several of the boundary stones are decorated with cup marks, shallow circular hollows that were pecked into the stone, probably with another stone. There are similar cup marks in other megalithic

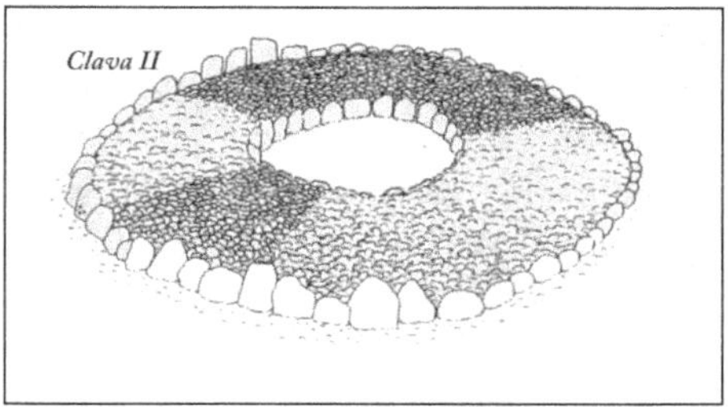

Clava II showing the four bands of contrasting stones.

sites throughout Scotland, especially near Kilmartin Glen (see p. 11). No one knows the significance of these marks, but they were obviously meaningful to the builders of these sites.

Elyn Aviva

Clava II today

The Clava Cairns are described as tombs, but it is clear to us that they had a significance far beyond the burial of the dead. They were used as burial sites, but that may have been because these places were of supreme importance to those who built them. They may have honored their departed relatives and friends by placing their remains at the ceremonial center of their community. We see churches and cathedrals that have been used in this way in more recent times,

An artist's impression of how Clava I might have appeared when first completed. (Aaron Watson)

> ". . . a megalith in a rural setting, in fields or woods, always has a distinctive atmosphere and character about it. The same tomb changes and alters its character according to the weather conditions, the qualities of light, the seasons of the year. It is never the same place twice. Such tombs are nowadays best seen alone: a crowd destroys the sense of place, the relationship between the tomb and its setting in the landscape." C. Tilly. "Art, Architecture, Landscape." In *Landscape: Politics and Perspectives,* edited by Barbara Bender. Providence/Oxford: Berg Publishers, 1994.

and no one would describe a cathedral as a tomb.

This site, nestled as it is in a grove of mature beech trees, creates an atmosphere of peace and encourages contemplation. The site was obviously recognized as a powerful place 4000 years ago and it retains that feeling today. Historical Scotland, which maintains the site, has been very sensitive and has intruded very little on the quiet atmosphere. Take some time to be nurtured by this ancient sacred site. Perhaps you will make contact with some of your distant relatives. They have much to teach you.

Battlefield of Culloden

The nearby Battlefield of Culloden is a National Trust of Scotland site, featuring a visitors' center and walks over the historic battlefield. The battle of Culloden took place on April 16th, 1746, between the British Crown forces and the Scottish Jacobites, led by Bonnie Prince Charlie. The Jacobites were defeated by the Duke of Cumberland, with heavy losses to their forces; some 1200 people were reputedly killed. The battle of Culloden ended the war of succession to the throne of Great Britain. Prince Charlie was forced to

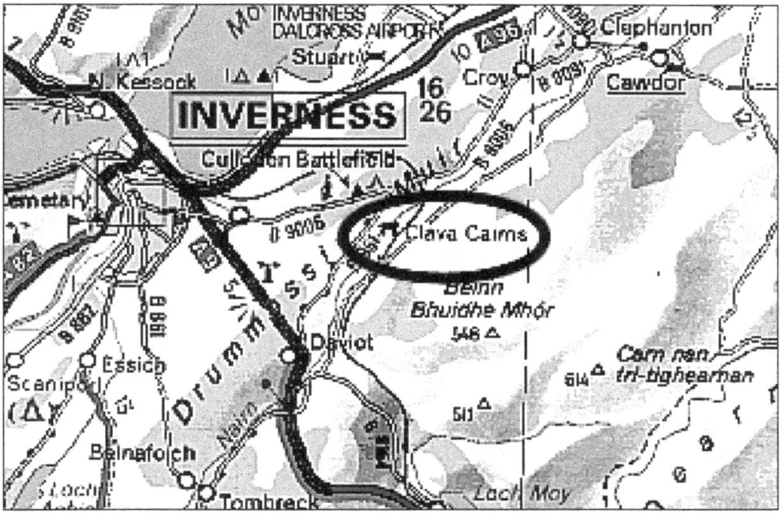

flee the field and make a desperate journey to France. This journey brought Charlie everlasting fame, and from this journey comes the romance and myth that are still associated with his failed cause.

Visiting the Clava Cairns

The site is open to the public without fee at all reasonable hours. A parking area is provided just outside the grounds. (http://www.megalithics.com/scotland/clavas/clavmain.htm) A descriptive brochure is available in the bookstore at Culloden.

Getting There

Balnuaran of Clava is located in Strathnairn, five miles east-south-east of Inverness, a mile southeast of the battlefield of Culloden and about six miles from Fort George (another Historic Scotland site).

Notes

Elyn Aviva

The Ring of Brodgar, Heart of Neolithic Orkney World Heritage Site

Maeshowe (Maes Howe) and the Heart of Neolithic Orkney World Heritage Site, Mainland, Orkney

We weren't there at the winter solstice sunset, when a shaft of sunlight pierces deep into the back of the chamber of Maeshowe, but the huge, turf-covered Stone Age cairn was still quite impressive. After crawling through the low passageway, a group of 18 of us stood inside without crowding. We examined the Viking runes (twelfth-century graffiti), the three empty cells opening onto the main chamber, and the superbly corbelled roof high above. Why, I wondered, do archeologists always call these cairns burial chambers? That's like calling Westminster Cathedral a tomb just because some people are buried there. I sensed that much more had happened here—for one thing, ongoing ceremony centering on the return of light after the shortest day of the year. We know so little and assume so much. Just because we are ignorant, we assume our ancestors were as well! (Elyn)

Maeshowe is the centerpiece of the Heart of Neolithic Orkney World Heritage Site. So designated in 1999 by UNESCO, the site also includes the Ring of Brodgar, the Watchstone, the Stones of Stenness, the Ring of Bookan Henge, and the Neolithic village of Skara Brae. It is one of the richest archeological sites in the world. We will concentrate on Maeshowe because we believe it is a particularly powerful place, but the entire

Elyn Aviva

Maeshowe

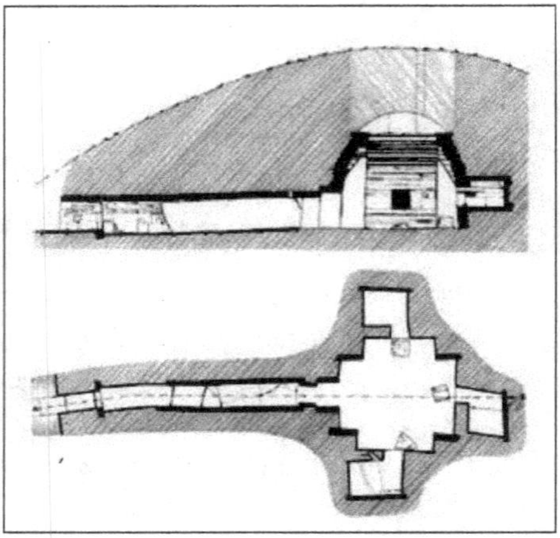

Cross section and plan of Maeshowe

complex makes a rewarding visit.

Maeshowe was built over 5000 years ago by the same Neolithic people who built many other sites all over Europe. There is enough similarity in construction among these sites to conclude that they were built by people who lived during the same time period and may have been in communication with each other. It is a so-called passage tomb, covered with earth, similar to those at Newgrange (Brú na Bóinne) in Ireland and the tumulae in Brittany in France. An outstanding feature of Maeshowe is its size. Though smaller than Brú na Bóinne, the mound is an impressive 115 feet in diameter and 24 feet high. (Brú na Bóinne is 250 feet across and 40 feet in height.) The

"The foundations of the interest in Earth Mysteries are the ancient sacred sites themselves. They call to us from the wild places of the Earth, and from the depths of time, confronting us like half-forgotten dreams. They tantalize us with their mystery, and provoke our imagination, telling of a former world that contained different ways of thinking and being. It may be during a brief visit to picturesque temple ruins while on holiday, or in an encounter with a gaunt standing stone when rambling on a windswept moor, but if the old places call to you, my advice is that you would do well to listen." Paul Devereux. *Earth Mysteries.* London: Judy Piatkus Ltd., 1999, p. 20.

central chamber is reached by a low, 36-foot-long entrance passage. The ceiling of the central chamber is 12.5 feet high and may have been higher originally. Three small chambers are located off the main chamber and are reached through doorways in each of the interior walls. A distinctive feature of these side chambers is that they are elevated above the level of the floor of the main chamber.

Some of the runic writings left by Vikings in Maeshowe

The first "modern" use of Maeshowe was by the Vikings in 1153. A party of men led by Earl Harald took refuge in the ancient structure, entering through the roof to wait out a severe storm. While they waited they carved runic graffiti on the walls. Translations of some of these inscriptions indicate they are similar in content to sexual graffiti found in

The sun entering Maeshowe at winter solstice

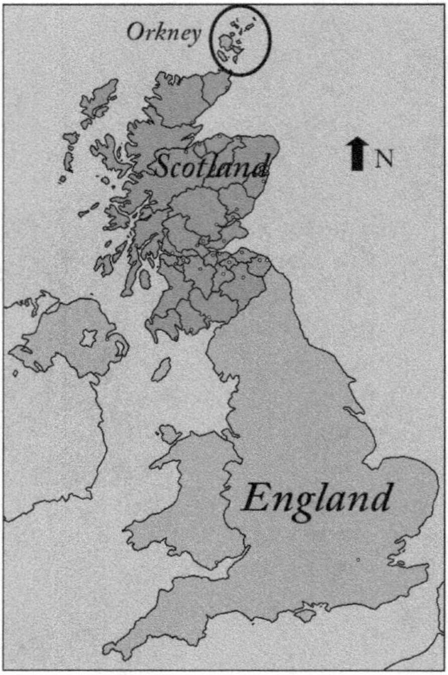

Map showing the Orkney Islands in relation to the rest of the UK

contemporary public toilets. The runic writing on the walls of Maeshowe is the largest collection found to date. Later, a different group of travelers, either returning from or going to the Crusades, spent some time in Maeshowe and also left their marks on the walls.

When the mound was excavated by James Farrer in 1861 the central chamber was entirely filled with debris. He and his workers broke through the roof and emptied the chamber. It was this group that discovered the earlier work of the Norsemen and Crusaders. It was also this unscientific nineteenth-century excavation that makes accurate dating of the site impossible. The estimates are based on the age of similar sites.

What was the original purpose of this "passage tomb"? It has long been known that the long passageway lines up with the setting sun at winter solstice, so an astronomical purpose is probable. Recent experiments with the acoustical properties of the central chamber seem to indicate that it may have been purposely designed to create unusual acoustical effects.

Drumming and chanting in certain places in the main chamber create the illusion that the sounds emanate from the side chambers. There is even a theory that all the sites in Orkney somehow mirror the constellation Orion. As with other megalithic monuments, there is no way of knowing exactly what the builders had in mind. Perhaps the site was a place of initiation and meditation. It certainly was for us. Since it is impossible to be alone or in silence in Maeshowe for any length of time, you will probably have to be content with a brief visit with others present.

Other Sites

The Heart of Neolithic Orkney monuments consist of Maeshowe, two ceremonial stone circles (the Stones of Stenness and the Ring of Brodgar), and a settlement (Skara Brae), together with a number of unexcavated burial, ceremonial, and settlement sites. The group constitutes a major prehistoric cultural landscape that provides information about life in this remote area 5000 years ago. The recent discovery of a huge structure (called a Neolithic "cathedral") measuring 82 feet by 65 feet located between the Stones of Stenness and the Ring of Brodgar is quite exciting. It promises to become the center of this group.

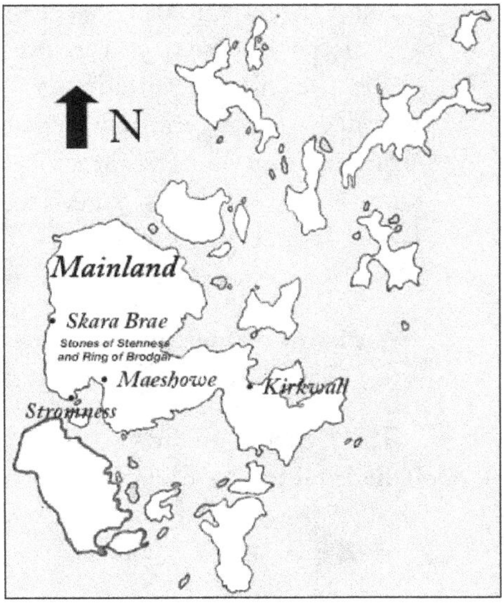

This reminds us of the importance of the intervisibility of megalithic sites. They need to be understood in relationship to each other.

The Stones of Stenness are on a promontory at the south bank of the stream that joins the southern ends of the seawater Loch of Stenness and the freshwater Loch of Harray. The name means "stone headland" in Old Norse. The stream is now bridged, but at one time it was crossed by a stepping-stone causeway. The Ring of Brodgar lies about 3/4 mile to the northwest, across the stream and near the tip of the isthmus formed between the two lochs. The Stones of Stenness have not been well cared for and only one third are still standing. Those that survive are impressive. The tallest is nearly 20 feet in height. The Ring of Brodgar, on the other hand, is more complete, but the stones are shorter in height. The Ring of Brodgar is 340 feet in diameter; the tallest of the stones are 15 feet in height.

Skara Brae is a large Neolithic settlement consisting of ten clustered houses preserved for 4000 years under the shifting sand dunes. A fierce storm in 1850 revealed the long-buried settlement. It was occupied from roughly 3100-2500 BCE and is Europe's most complete Neolithic village. This site was a deciding factor in naming the Heart of Neolithic Orkney a UNESCO World Heritage Site.

Visiting Maeshowe and the Heart of Neolithic Orkney World Heritage Site

The Heart of Neolithic Orkney World Heritage Site is maintained by Historic Scotland. It is necessary to book your visit to Maeshowe in advance and join one of the tours. Tour groups are limited to 20 persons, so you will need to choose a specific time for your visit. Ticket prices are quite reasonable. Visit their website at www.historic-scotland.gov.uk/

Getting There

Orkney (never "The Orkneys") is a group of over 70 islands, 20 of which are inhabited. The largest island, known as Mainland, (we find that a curious name for an island!) is the sixth largest island in Scotland. The largest settlement and the administrative center of Orkney is Kirkwall, Mainland. Flights to Kirkwall are available from Aberdeen, Glasgow, Edinburgh, and Inverness. Local transport can be arranged from Kirkwall. A number of local guide services are available. There is also an auto/passenger ferry link to Mainland Orkney, from Scrabster to Stromness. Check with Northlink Ferry (www.northlinkferries.co.uk/) for departures. A number of companies offer packages that include transport, lodging, and admission to the sites. Google "Tours to Orkney" and you will see what is available.

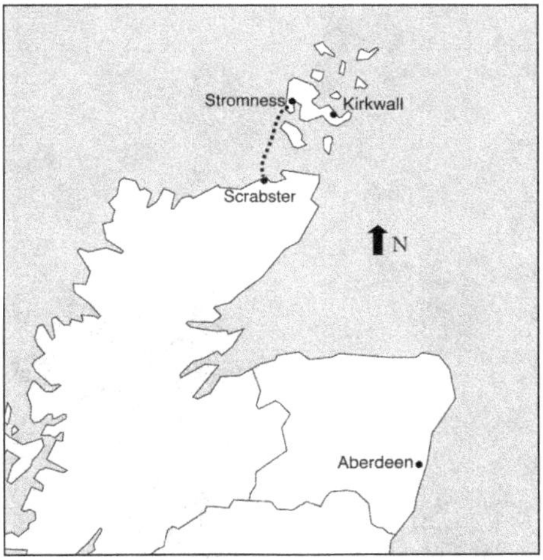

Auto/passenger ferry from Scrabster to Stromness

Elyn Aviva

The tall trees in Diana's Grove

Diana's Grove, Blair Castle, Perthshire

Wandering through Diana's Grove, I felt as if I were in a magical wilderness surrounded by immense, wise elders—beings more commonly known as "trees." But to call these graceful beings "trees" doesn't do them justice. Huge (some more than 170 feet high), exotic (Grand Fir, Noble Fir, Douglas Fir, Larch, Western Hemlock, and Wellingtonia stand out), and magnificent, they were carefully planted over 100 years ago in a landscaped "wilderness" originally laid out in 1737.

The dappled grove provides a proper setting for the statue of Diana—goddess of the hunt, fertility, and the moon—in the center. I wondered whether on moonlit nights Diana steps off her pedestal, unstrings her bow, and takes a stroll to the nearby ruined chapel of St. Bridget. Idle thoughts? Perhaps not. (Elyn)

Diana's Grove is on the grounds of Blair Castle, the most-visited historic house in Scotland. The grove is a unique stand of very tall conifers that were carefully planted in the late nineteenth century by the seventh Duke of Atholl, John Stewart Murray, after a devastating storm in 1893 laid many of the earlier plantings low. The Duke scoured the world for exotic varieties of evergreen trees and brought them together in an easily walkable two-acre grove. An-

"We Celts are lovers of trees. In fact, the religion of our primal ancestors is one truly rooted in the mysticism of the trees. From old Celtic tales that speak of First Man being an alder tree, and First Woman being a rowan tree, to the ancient Roman accounts of the Druids in the groves of old Gaul, trees play a central role in the ancient Celtic way of seeing." Frank MacEowen. *The Mist-Filled Path*. Novato, CA: New World Library, 2002, p. 10.

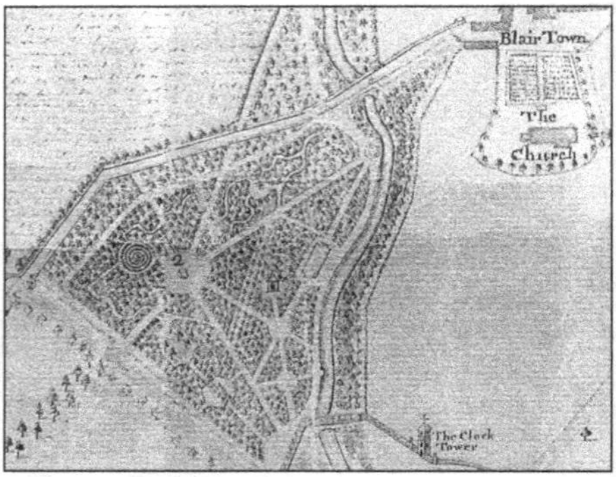

Diana's Grove in a survey by James Dorret in 1758

other storm in 2001 blew down fourteen of the largest trees. The opening created by these losses provides a vantage point to fully appreciate the grandeur of those that survive. These very tall trees produce an atmosphere rich in oxygen that refreshes the body and clears the mind. Just to step into such an atmosphere is like a visit to a spa!

Even more healing is the living presence of the trees, which incite awe and wonder and invites our participation in all that is vital and growing in our world. To meditate in this place is to receive wisdom from some of the largest, oldest, and wisest of our fellow creatures. Listen to what they may be whispering to you. It will not be expressible in words, but you will feel it in your soul.

Diana, goddess of the hunt

In the very center of the grove you will find the statue of Diana, after whom

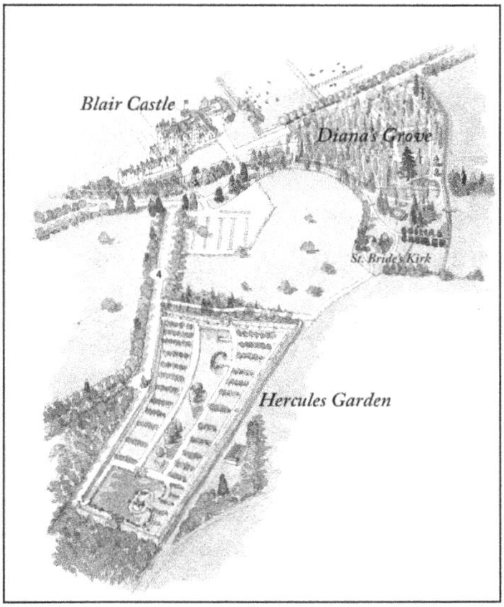

Diana's Grove and Hercules Garden

the grove is named. The paths are arranged to allow viewing of the statue from the castle itself.

Just south of the grove is the private burial ground for previous Dukes of Atholl, near St. Bride's Kirk. This thirteenth-century church is a picturesque ruin and a reminder of St. Bride's presence here on the mainland (See pp. 43-47).

Diana's Grove is part of Perthshire's Big Tree Country project, which is the center of a worldwide effort to save these wonderful trees from ruthless exploitation and destruction by commercial interests. You can visit their website at: http://www.perthshirebigtreecountry.co.uk/ to learn more and offer your support for their efforts. You can also make a donation to plant a tree to support replanting the ancient Caledonian forest at www.treesforlife.org.uk. This latter project includes a variety of trees.

Elyn Aviva

St. Bride's Kirk

We suggest that you purchase one of the small guides to the grove that are sold at the castle gift shop. One guide lists all the major trees in the grove by height, girth, and species, and a small booklet details the history of the grove.

If you appreciate more formal gardens, Blair Castle also has the magnificent Hercules Garden, a walled enclosure of nine acres that has been carefully restored

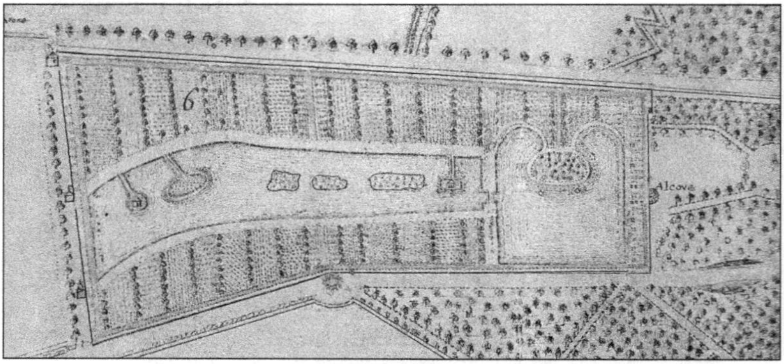

James Dorret's 1758 survey of Hercules Garden

to its original 1746 plan. The history of this garden is contained in the booklet described above.

Visiting Diana's Grove

The entrance to Diana's Grove is through a gate that is visible from the castle steps. Look to your left when facing away from the castle and you will see it. Physically challenged visitors can tour Diana's Grove by renting a limited mobility scooter provided by the castle. Inquire at the castle entrance hall for information about this option.

Blair Castle contains a spectacular display of arms and armor in the main entrance hall. The extensive

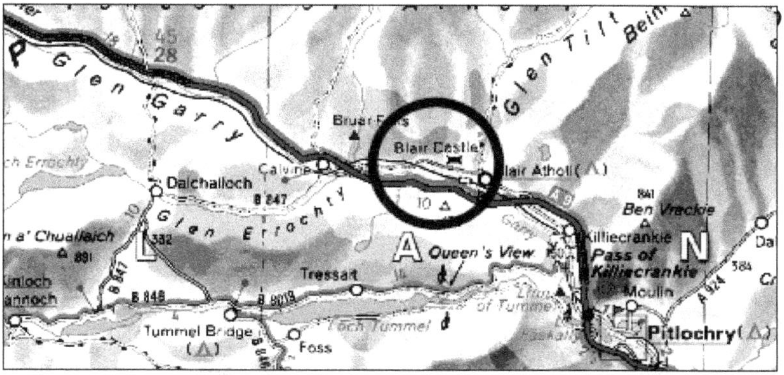

Area map

collections also include paintings, furniture, porcelain, embroidery, Masonic regalia, and family memorabilia. The Atholl Highlander Room commemorates Europe's only remaining private army, which has its headquarters at the castle. An audiovisual display provides a general overview of the castle.

The ticket booth is at the entrance to the grounds and castle. A "grounds only" admission costs approximately half as much as visiting both the castle and grounds. If you want to combine a visit to Diana's Grove with a visit to the castle, you should purchase the combined ticket at the entrance. Inquire about open hours before your visit at http://www.blair-castle.co.uk/.

Next to the gift shop at the castle is the Tullibardine Restaurant, which is a good place to take a light meal or snack.

Getting There

Blair Castle and Diana's Grove are 35 miles north of Perth just off the main Perth/Inverness highway (A9). Blair Atholl Station has regular train services from all major Scottish cities, from which you can easily reach the castle.

Elyn Aviva

The nemeton in Roslin Glen

Rosslyn Chapel and Roslin Glen, Lothian

We'd been to Rosslyn Chapel several times before, and each time the amount of scaffolding seemed to have multiplied. This time it had encroached on the inside of the chapel, blocking from view the star- and moon-encrusted vaulted ceiling. The interior scaffolding markedly changed the atmosphere within. But even so, much of the puzzling symbolism remains visible: evocative carvings of New World vegetation before the New World was discovered; open and closed books and scrolls; angels pointing toward crosses or hanging upside down, bound in ropes; two knights riding a single horse; a man holding a rope around another's neck while the bound man kneels; grimacing skulls and benign faces; protruding cubes covered with geometric patterns; prolific Green Men, vines spewing from their mouths—and of course, the famous twin pillars of the Master Mason and the Apprentice, the latter pillar evoking the Scandinavian World Tree, Yggrasil, its base sculpted with eight serpents.... Go figure.

Better to retreat to the woods, to Roslin Glen, a Celtic nemeton of old, a sacred clearing in the forest surrounded by ancient yew, chestnut, beech, and sycamore trees. Water flows nearby. We stand still and listen.... (Elyn)

Roslin (or Rosslyn) Glen is the largest surviving tract of ancient woodland in the area. Deep in the valley there is evidence of Bronze Age settlement. So perhaps it is no surprise to find a nemeton—along with a waterfall, a small cave (sometimes linked with Gawain of Arthurian legend), and rocks covered with Ogham script and spiral carvings.

Early picture of Rosslyn Chapel with Roslin Castle in the glen below

A nemeton is a sacred space associated with the ancient Celtic religion. Nemeta are primarily situated in natural areas and often were sacred groves, but the term may originally have also referred to shrines and temples.

To find the nemeton in Roslin Glen (it is not marked on any tourist map), walk up the paved lane past Rosslyn chapel to the Caravan Club. Take the smaller lane to the right and turn off on the trail to the right. You will reach the glen after a short walk. The central clearing and surrounding yew trees (the nemeton) are obvious. Some of the yews appear to be bleeding. They exude a dark red sap, which may be caused by a fungus. There are the remains of a stone wall at the back of the clearing. The path turns sharply just beyond this wall and leads down toward the river, eventually leading to the castle and back up to the chapel.

Take time to absorb the atmosphere of the glen and visit some of the trees. Listen to the sounds of flowing water and breathe in the atmosphere of this place. Some believe that the glen is the source of energy that feeds

Captain John Slezer's drawing of Rosslyn Chapel in the late seventeenth century

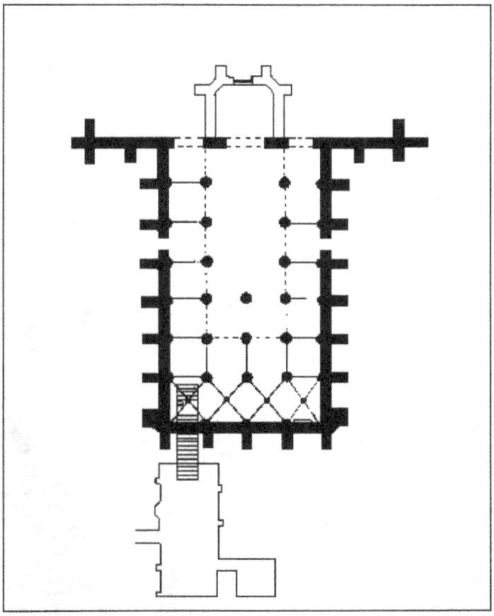

Floor plan of the chapel

the chapel—water flowing out of underground caverns, energy swirling up, making its way from glen to chapel.

The central clearing is a perfect place to do a meditation or a ritual. Since it is not marked on any map, the nemeton remains in nearly pristine condition. Remember ECOLOGY and leave this place just as you found it. After a walk to the glen you may find yourself better prepared to view the chapel itself, encased as it is in scaffolding.

Rosslyn Chapel

Rosslyn Chapel was founded in 1446 by William Sinclair, the third Earl of Orkney. Originally intended as the choir of a much larger collegiate church, construc-

Historic engraving of the interior of the chapel showing the Apprentice's Column on the right

tion stopped on the death of its founder. You can still see the outlines of the original church marked in the ground west of the chapel. The only evidence of these original plans is the large exterior wall that projects outward from the western façade of the building.

Another engraving of the interior of the chapel showing the entrance and side aisle

The exterior and interior of the sandstone chapel contain an amazing variety of intricate carvings, many of which have connections to the Masonic Order, including several drawing-compass carvings, which is a primary symbol of the Masons. Several angels in the chapel are in postures that are said to relate to initiation rituals of First Degree Freemasonry.

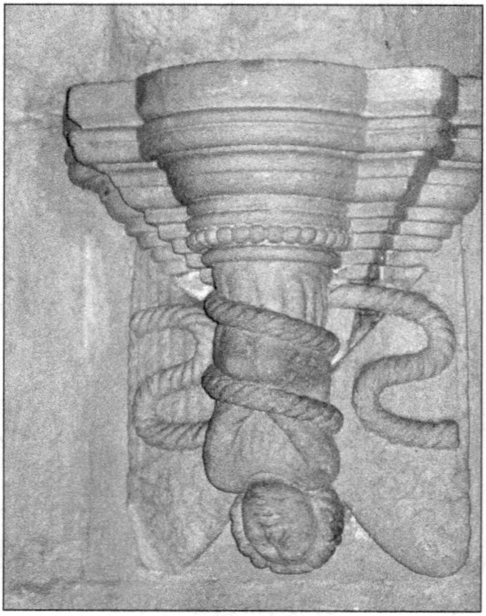

Elyn Aviva

Detail of a capital

A number of other mysteries are

Elyn Aviva

Ceiling of the chapel

associated with the chapel, including carvings that closely resemble plants in the North American continent. These carvings predate the introduction of these plants to Europe from the New World, giving rise to theories of successful voyages before Columbus. References to the Knights Templar are also found by many people, in spite of the fact that the Templars were supposedly disbanded in 1312, well before the construction of the chapel. Mysteries abound, as numerous as the carvings on the walls.

A disastrous restoration in the 1950s nearly brought the entire sandstone structure to the ground. The interior of the chapel was sealed with a thin coat of plaster, which had the effect of trapping moisture in the stone. This impending catastrophe was only discovered when small piles of sand began to dribble onto the floor at various points inside the building. The sandstone was literally disintegrating. The solution, which will take many years to accomplish, was to build a temporary roof over the entire structure and allow the trapped moisture to gradually escape. Current plans are to remove the interior sealer coat and stabilize the stones. Only time will tell if this restoration will be successful.

Rosslyn Chapel is a powerful place and you can experience this power in spite of the thousands of tourists who storm through it each year because of the popularity of *The DaVinci Code*. You can still feel the energy of the place despite the extensive ongoing restoration efforts. This may be due to the flow of energy from the river that continues to feed the chapel.

Roslin Castle as it would have appeared when new

If you would like to visit Roslin Castle, take the marked path past the entrance to the visitors' center. There has been a castle on this site since the early fourteenth century, when the Sinclair family built a fortification. Following its destruction during the Anglo-Scottish wars in the sixteenth century, the castle was rebuilt. This structure, built into the cliffs of Rosslyn Glen, has remained at least partially inhabited ever since. The castle is accessed via a high bridge, which replaced an earlier drawbridge. Roslin Castle was renovated in the 1980s and now serves as holiday accommodations. You can continue beyond the castle into the depths of the glen and approach the nemeton from the other side.

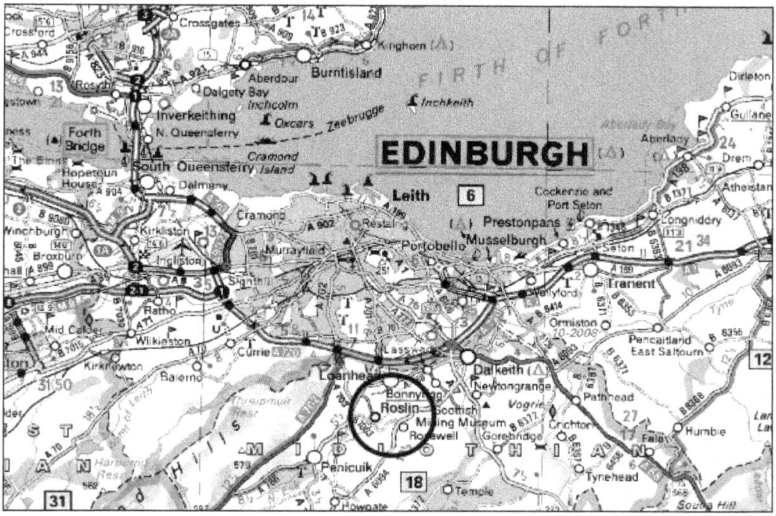

Map of the area

Visiting Rosslyn Chapel

The visitors' center at the entrance to the chapel grounds charges an admission fee. You should check in advance about open hours. Roslin Glen is open to the public with no admission fee. (http://www.undiscoveredscotland.co.uk/roslin/rosslynchapel/ and http://walking scotland.com/walks/centralscotland/roslin-glen)

Getting There

The village of Roslin is seven miles south of central Edinburgh, located just off Edinburgh's City Bypass, south of Loanhead and east of Penicuik. It can be reached by bus from Edinburgh or as part of a bus tour from the city. (Many tours include visits to Rosslyn Chapel.) There is a parking lot in front of the visitors' center and a visitors' car park next to the old Roslin Inn, fifty yards away from the chapel. A charming B&B is located down a lane across from Rosslyn Chapel, if you prefer to stay really close.

Afterword

We hope you have enjoyed this brief tour of powerful places in Scotland and will choose to visit some of them. If you do, you'll discover the special qualities of the different islands—the tranquil isolation of Mull, the "out on the edge" feel of Lewis, the meditative landscape of Iona—to name a few. You will find Scottish hospitality is first-rate, and you will be met with courteous and helpful people wherever you go. Scotland offers the transformational traveler a multitude of unique experiences that compensate for the challenges the rugged terrain provides.

In this guide we have described only powerful places that we have visited. We know of others that would be worthwhile exploring, including the Eildon Hills, St. Cuthbert's Way from Melrose Abbey to the Holy Island of Lindisfarne, Glen Lyon (the Valley of the Sun God), the ancient shrine called the House of the Old Woman (Tigh Na Cailliche) far back in the glen near Fortingall, and the fairy mountain of Schiehallion. Perhaps another time. You may find others yourself. If so, let us know. We are always looking forward to the next adventure!

Glossary

BCE Before the Common Era (contemporary replacement for BC, which stands for Before Christ).

blind spring Underground water feature that has not broken through to the surface.

Bronze Age An age that began with metalworking, specifically the smelting of copper and tin to make bronze. Introduced in Scotland just before 2000 BCE (in Britain overall, the Bronze Age lasted from 2100–750 BCE). Associated with various types of cairns, sometimes built inside Neolithic henges or tombs.

cairn A man-made pile of stones, often in a conical form. They may be of recent construction or very old. Also refers to a megalithic tomb covered with small stones. Those we describe in this book were constructed in Neolithic times.

CE Common Era (contemporary replacement for AD, which stands for *Anno Domini*—in the year of the Lord).

Celt A nineteenth-century term used to describe any of the European peoples who spoke, or speak, a Celtic language. The term is also used in a wider sense to describe the modern descendants of those peoples, notably those who participate in a Celtic culture. A member of a group of Indo-Europeans found in Germany and France in the Second Millennium BCE. The six territories recognized by the Celtic League and Celtic Congress as Celtic Nations are Brittany, Cornwall, Ireland, Isle of Man, Scotland, and Wales. Limiting the territories to these six is disputed by people from England, Asturias and Galicia in Spain, and several other European countries that also retain some Celtic cultural traits. Celts settled in Scotland beginning around 1000 BCE.

Celtic cross A symbol that combines a cross with a circle surrounding the intersection.

crofter A British farmer who has the use of a small fenced area of land.

cross-quarter days A day falling approximately halfway between a solstice and an equinox; they were important feast days in traditional Celtic societies.

Cup and ring marks Stone-picked designs of hollowed-out cups and rings, often concentric. Thought to date to late Neolithic or Bronze Age. Found on megaliths and also on slabs of bedrock. Purpose unknown.

Dalriada An ancient Gaelic kingdom on the western seaboard of Scotland with some territory on the northern coasts of Ireland. In the late sixth and early seventh centuries it encompassed roughly what is now Argyll, Bute, and Lochaber in Scotland and County Antrim in Northern Ireland.

dolmen A type of single-chamber megalithic (large stone) construction, usually consisting of three or more upright stones supporting a large flat horizontal capstone. Most date from the early Neolithic period (4000-3000 BCE). They are often called tombs, but that may not be an accurate or complete description. Often what remains today is the stone "skeleton," which resembles a table, but originally the structure was covered with earth or stones.

Druid A member of the priestly and learned class active in Gaul, and perhaps in Celtic culture more generally, during the final centuries BCE and until the thorough Christianization of Celtic peoples in Scotland and Ireland. Their teachings were passed down orally and so very little is known about them.

Gaia A name for Mother Earth. The Gaia hypothesis proposes that the biosphere and the physical components of the Earth are closely integrated to form a complex interacting system. The hypothesis is frequently described as viewing the Earth as a single organism.

geomancer A practitioner of geomancy.

geomancy An art that analyses the subtle earth energies that ebb and flow throughout the landscape, influencing health and wealth; home, garden and office alike.

glen A valley, typically one that is long, deep, and often U-shaped; or one with a watercourse running through such a valley. The word comes from the Irish/Scottish Gaelic word *gleann*, or *glion* in Manx.

Green Man A sculpture or drawing of a (usually) male face surrounded by or made from leaves. Branches or vines may sprout from the nose, mouth, nostrils or other parts of the face. Green Man motifs are found from the second and third century in the Rhineland and, more particularly, in twelfth-century and later European art.

Hebrides The Hebrides comprise a widespread and diverse group of islands off the west coast of Scotland. There are two main groups: the Inner and Outer Hebrides.

henge A large, nearly circular or oval prehistoric earthworks composed of a boundary ditch and an external bank.

Heraclitus A pre-Socratic Greek philosopher (c. 535-475 BCE), a native of Ephesus on the coast of Asia Minor. He was of distinguished parentage and regarded himself as self-taught and a pioneer of wisdom.

hill fort A type of fortified refuge or defended settlement, located to exploit a rise in elevation for defensive advantage. They are typically European and of the Bronze and Iron Ages.

Ice Age A geological period of long-term reduction in the temperature of the Earth's surface and atmosphere, resulting in an expansion of continental ice sheets, polar ice sheets, and alpine glaciers. The last Ice Age ended around 10,000 years ago in Europe.

Iron Age The period during which tools and weapons were primarily made of iron or steel, replacing bronze. The period began in Scotland around 700 BCE. There is a paucity of evidence of burials but much evidence of defensive and domestic sites.

megalith A large stone which has been used to construct a structure or monument, either alone or together with other stones. Megalithic means structures made of such large stones, utilizing an interlocking system without the use of mortar or cement. They date from 4500-1500 BCE in Europe.

Mesolithic period Middle Stone Age, the period between the end of the Paleolithic and the beginning of the Neolithic. Began with the end of the last glacial period over 10,000 years ago. Mesolithic culture involved the gradual domestication of plants and animals and the formation of settled communities but relied mostly on hunting, fishing, and food gathering. Mesolithic cultures lasted in Europe until almost 3000 BCE.

nemeton A sacred space utilized in Celtic religion. Nemeta appear to have been primarily situated in natural areas, and often centered around trees; as such they are often described as sacred groves. Nemeton is related to the name of the Nemates tribe of what is now Germany and to the goddess Nemetona.

Neolithic The New Stone Age. A period in the development of human technology, beginning about 4000 BCE in Scotland. It is traditionally considered the last period of the Stone Age. The Neolithic people were farmers who domesticated plants and animals and created pottery and woven textiles. They built numerous constructions, including dolmens, stone circles, and earthen henges and erected many standing stones.

Ogham script An ancient form of writing, found exclusively in Ireland, Scotland, and Wales, dating around the 3rd to 6th century CE.

passage tomb A megalithic site usually dating to the Neolithic. Some have simple single chambers, while others have sub-chambers leading off from the main chamber. They were entered via a covered passageway. They are called tombs but also served other ceremonial purposes.

Picts An ancient people of uncertain origin who inhabited parts of northern Britain, fought against the Romans, and in the 9th century CE united with the Scots.

scriptorium A room in a monastery set aside for the copying, writing, or illuminating of manuscripts and records.

Sheela-na-gig Figurative carvings of (often skeletal) naked women displaying exaggerated genitalia. They are found on churches, castles, and other buildings, particularly in the British Isles, dating approximately from the 11th to 16th centuries.

"thin place" A place (in nature or in a human construction) where the veil between this world and other realms (fairy, the Other World, etc.) is thin and passage between our normal consensual reality and a different kind of reality is more easily accomplished.

tumulus A mound of earth and stones raised over a dolmen. Often referred to as a tomb, but served as more than a burial site.

Western Isles The Outer Hebrides, an island chain off the west coast of Scotland. Scottish Gaelic was formerly the dominant language and remains widely spoken even though some areas are now English speaking.

Bibliography

(This list includes books cited in this guidebook as well as books of interest)

Aviva, Elyn. *Walking Through Cancer: A Pilgrimage of Gratitude on the Way of St. James*. Santa Fe: Pilgrims Process, Inc., 2009.

Burke, John, and Kaj Halberg. *Seed of Knowledge, Stone of Plenty: Understanding the Lost Technology of the Ancient Megalith-Builders*. San Francisco: Council Oak Books, 2005.

Burl, Aubrey. *A Guide to the Stone Circles of Britain, Ireland and Brittany*. New Haven: Yale University Press, 1995.

Coppens, Philip. *The Stone Puzzle of Rosslyn Chapel: The Truth behind Its Templar and Masonic Secrets.* Enkhuizen, the Netherlands: Frontier Publishing, 2004.

Devereux, Paul. *Earth Memory: Sacred Sites—Doorways into Earth's Mysteries.* St. Paul, MN: Llewellyn Publications, 1992.

———. *Earth Mysteries.* London: Judy Piatkus (Publishers) Ltd, 1999.

———. *Places of Power: Secret Energies at Ancient Sites: A Guide to Observed or Measured Phenomena*. London: Blandford, 1990.

———. *Re-Visioning the Earth: A Guide to Opening the Healing Channels Between Mind and Nature*. New York: Fireside, 1996.

——— *The Sacred Place: The Ancient Origin of Holy and Mystical Sites.* London: Cassel & Co., 2000.

Freeman, Mara. *Kindling the Celtic Spirit: Ancient Traditions to Illumine Your Life Throughout the Seasons*. New York: HarperSanFrancisco, a division of HarperCollins Publishers Inc., 2001.

Furlong, David. *Working with Earth Energies: How to Tap into the Healing Powers of the Natural World.* London: Judy Piatkus (Publishers) Ltd, 2003.

Graves, Tom. *Needles of Stone Revisited.* Glastonbury: Gothic Image Publications, 1986.

Gray, William G. *By Standing Stone & Elder Tree: Ritual and the Unconscious.* St. Paul, MN: Llewellyn Publications, 1990.

Heselton, Philip. *Earth Mysteries.* Shaftsbury, Dorset: Element Books Ltd, 1995.

Holder, Geoff. *The Guide to Mysterious Iona and Staffa.* Stroud, Gloucestershire: Tempus Publishing Ltd, 2007.

Kelly, Eamonn P. *Sheela-na-Gigs: Origins and Functions.* Country House, Dublin, in association with the National Museum of Ireland, 1996.

Lonegren, Sig. *Spiritual Dowsing*. Glastonbury: Gothic Image Publications, 1996.

MacDonald, Jonathan. *Discovering Skye: A Handbook of the Island's History and Legend.* Kilmuir, Skye: J. MacDonald, n.d.

MacEowen, Frank. *The Mist-Filled Path: Celtic Wisdom for Exiles, Wanderers, and Seekers.* Novato, CA: New World Library, 2002.

MacSween, Ann. *A Wee Guide to Prehistoric Scotland.* Musselburgh, Scotland: Goblinshead, 2005.

Matthews, John. *The Green Man.* Newburyport, MA: Red Wheel/Weiser, Book and Access edition, 2002.

Pennick, Nigel. *Celtic Sacred Landscapes.* New York: Thames & Hudson Inc., 1996.

Pogacnik, Marko. *Sacred Geography: Geomancy: Co-Creating the Earth Cosmos.* Great Barrington, MA: Lindisfarne Books, 2007.

Queally, Jackie. *The Spiritual Meaning of Rosslyn's Carvings: A Journey round the Chapel.* Roslin: published by the author, 2007.

Richardson, Alan. *Spirits of the Stones.* London: Virgin, 2001.

Swire, Otta. *Skye: The Island and Its Legends.* Edinburgh: Birlinn Ltd, 2006.

Tilly, C. "Art, Architecture, Landscape." In *Landscape: Politics and Perspectives,* edited by Barbara Bender. Providence/Oxford: Berg Publishers, 1994.

Wallace-Murphy, Tim. *Cracking the Symbol Code: Revealing the Secret Heretical Messages within Church and Renaissance Art.* London: Watkins Publishing, 2005.

CPSIA information can be obtained
at www.ICGtesting.com
Printed in the USA
BVHW061601070222
628203BV00002B/344

9 780982 623305